iPod® and iTunes® Digital Field Guide

D1507981

iPod® and iTunes® Digital Field Guide

Chad Fahs

WILEY

Wiley Publishing, Inc.

iPod® and iTunes® Digital Field Guide

Published by
Wiley Publishing, Inc.
111 River Street
Hoboken, N.J. 07030
www.wiley.com

WILEY

About the Author

Chad Fahs is an author whose work includes *HDV Filmmaking, Final Cut Pro 4 For Dummies, MacWorld DVD Studio Pro Bible, Flash MX Design for TV and Video, Apple Pro Training Series: DVD Studio Pro 2,* and *Mac OS X Panther in Ten Simple Steps or Less*. In addition, Chad has been an instructor in the Multimedia Arts department at the College of DuPage (located outside of Chicago, IL). He is also a certified Apple instructor and has taught classes and custom courses in Final Cut Pro and DVD Studio Pro for Future Media Concepts in Philadelphia, PA, and Washington, D.C. Chad also writes, directs, produces, edits, and consults for a variety of projects and clients. He is currently an editor at Concrete Pictures in the Philadelphia area.

Credits

Acquisitions Editor
Michael Roney

Project Editor
Cricket Krengel

Technical Editor
John C. Welch

Editorial Contributor
Dennis R. Cohen

Copy Editor
Elizabeth Kuball

Editorial Manager
Robyn Siesky

Vice President & Group Executive Publisher
Richard Swadley

Vice President & Publisher
Barry Pruett

Project Coordinator
Maridee Ennis

Graphics and Production Specialists
Carrie A. Foster
Lauren Goddard
Denny Hager
Jennifer Heleine
Clint Lahnen

Quality Control Technician
Laura Albert

Cover Design
Michael Trent

Proofreading and Indexing
Vicki Broyles
Rebecca R. Plunkett

I would like to dedicate this book to my sister Pia and my niece Kara, who was born while I was writing this book. Wishing you both a long life full of happiness and music.

Acknowledgments

I would like to acknowledge the efforts of my editors Mike Roney and Cricket Krengel for the completion of this book. I would also like to thank my agent David Fugate at Waterside Productions for his continual assistance. In addition, I would like to thank all of my family and friends who have inspired and supported me throughout the years, including during the time spent writing this book. Finally, thank you to Dennis R. Cohen for his editorial contributions.

Preface

The iPod is the quintessential digital music player for today's generation, much as the portable cassette and CD players (led by Sony's Walkman) influenced others in past decades. Small, stylish, and simple to use, it is the essence of Apple's design philosophy.

By expanding on the portability of mobile devices and making music more accessible, devices like Apple's iPod have changed the rules and opened up new possibilities for collectors and distributors everywhere. The recent success of legally downloaded music, as well as the seemingly endless growth of iPod popularity, point to a future where more of the music you purchase and listen to will exist solely in the digital realm.

With the ability to carry an entire music library in your pocket, Apple's iPod has forever altered the music landscape. This book serves as an introduction and guide to this amazing device, including its related software and accessories (of which there are many). Hopefully, this will instruct and inspire you to learn more about the iPod, whether you are already an owner or are seriously considering a purchase.

Just remember that in the end, despite the really cool technology at your fingertips, it's really about the music.

Contents at a Glance

Contents

Chapter 3: iPod Basics and More   39

Part II: Working with iPod Software   57

Chapter 4: iTunes Basics and More   59

Chapter 5: iTunes Music Store 119

Part III: Getting the Most Out of the iPod 135

Chapter 6: iPod Accessories 137

Chapter 7: Special Tips and Techniques 147

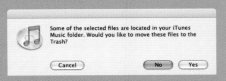

Chapter 8: iPod Maintenance and Troubleshooting 185

iPod

Do not disconnect.

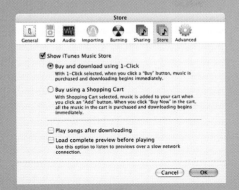

Quick Tour

QT

Welcome to the *iPod and iTunes Digital Field Guide.* This Quick Start chapter assumes that you're a new user who is looking for the quickest way to start using your new iPod, whether it's an iPod, iPod mini, iPod photo, iPod U2 Special Edition, or iPod shuffle. If you've already learned the basics for how to use an iPod, you can skip this Quick Start and proceed to the next chapter. However, if you're new to iPods and the world of portable digital music players, this chapter should quickly get you up to speed on the basics of the device, its controls, and methods for getting songs into it from your computer. Specifics for using the full potential of your iPod are covered in subsequent chapters of this book.

Although each iPod model has its own defining characteristics, the basics are generally the same. To begin, take a look at a few requirements for using your new iPod with a computer, which is required for transferring songs onto the device and managing your music collection.

What You Need

In order to use an iPod effectively, a few basic requirements must be met. These include a suitable computer, an Internet connection (optional), iTunes software, and the necessary cables to make connections.

Multimedia computer

First of all, you need a Mac or PC computer (desktop or laptop) to download or convert music files for use on your iPod. Without a computer, your iPod is basically useless (unless someone fills up the iPod with songs for you). Most computers that are multimedia-capable are suitable for working with an iPod and the iTunes software, which is the central hub that allows you to download, convert, and manage all the songs for your iPod. Make certain that your computer has a FireWire port (standard on all Macs made in the last several years) or a USB 2.0 port, which is the standard connection type for PCs (these ports are also available on recent Macs).

iTunes software

Make sure to install the iTunes software on your computer before proceeding any further. iTunes software ships in the box with new iPods and can be downloaded for free from the Apple Web site at www.apple.com/ilife/itunes. It's also a part of the new iLife series of applications for Apple, which includes iTunes, iPhoto, iMovie, iDVD, and GarageBand.

Internet connection

If you're downloading songs from the iTunes Music Store, you also need a fast Internet connection, preferably DSL or cable, although a dial-up connection might suffice if it's reliable and you're willing to wait a while to receive your song purchases. An Internet connection is also necessary to access a database of song titles, which makes automatically labeling your songs and CDs a snap.

Cables and connections

iPods ship with the necessary cables for connecting with your computer and charging the device. However, an optional Dock accessory is basically a cradle for quickly and easily working with your iPod without connecting and disconnecting wires. If you use your iPod a lot, you might consider purchasing the Dock accessory, unless it has already shipped in the box with your iPod. A few iPod models come standard with a Dock as an additional purchase incentive. Also, the iPod photo comes with a particularly special version of the Dock that is necessary for viewing photos and slideshows on a television set.

Charging the Battery

At this point you really should have read through the material that came with your specific iPod. But, if you haven't yet read this material, then you probably haven't charged your battery either. And, before using your iPod, you need to do this. So, connect the special FireWire cable you received with your iPod to the AC wall adapter that is included in the box. The first time you use your iPod, make sure to allow the device to fully charge before using it. This process may take a few hours, so be patient. As you'll learn, your iPod also charges through a FireWire or USB 2.0 port when it's attached to your computer during the process of transferring music.

Note *Although iPods interface with a computer through a FireWire or USB 2.0 port, the device is equipped with a special Dock Connector on the bottom, which is a thin type of connection specific to an iPod (with the exception of the iPod shuffle). Not just any FireWire or USB cable will suffice for connecting your iPod to the charger, your computer, or the Dock accessory. The cables that shipped with your iPod contain a FireWire or USB 2.0 connector on one end and a Dock connector on the other.*

1. **Open the iTunes application by clicking on its icon in the Applications folder (Mac) or locating it in the Start menu (PC).** If you're using a Mac, an icon may already be added to the Dock, and if you're on a PC an alias may have been created for you on the desktop.

iTunes

QT.1 The iTunes application is used to import songs and manage your music collection.

Importing Songs from an Audio CD

Before you can use your iPod, you need to import music into your computer using the iTunes software. Most users import music from a CD or through the iTunes Music Store. You may also bring in music from other sources, such as MP3s and other audio files already on your hard drive. (Additional audio formats and other methods for importing music, photos, and other files for your iPod are covered throughout this book.) Downloading songs from the iTunes Music Store for use on your iPod has become a popular option. An entire chapter in this book is dedicated to the iTunes Music Store, although for the purposes of this Quick Tour, I am assuming that you're importing music from an audio CD, although downloaded music operates the same in iTunes and on your iPod.

The following steps illustrate how to import music from an audio CD using the iTunes software.

2. **Insert an audio CD into your computer's CD-ROM or DVD-ROM drive.** iTunes automatically recognizes the CD, searches an Internet database for song titles (if you're online), imports the songs, and names them for you.

QT.2 iTunes automatically looks up song information for tracks you import from a CD.

QT.3 Use the Import button if iTunes doesn't automatically import the contents of a CD.

3. **Select the CD in the Source list on the left side of the iTunes application window if iTunes does not automatically import the songs (as described in Step 2).** Click the Import button, located in the upper-right corner of the application window.

in the box with your device. You may place the iPod in the special Dock accessory if it's connected to your computer. For users of the iPod shuffle, there is no need for extra cables. Simply remove the cap on the bottom of the iPod shuffle and plug it into an unused USB 2.0 port on your computer or keyboard (there is also a special Dock accessory available for the iPod shuffle).

Connecting the iPod to Your Computer

Cross-Reference *For more information about the various accessories available for your iPod, see Chapter 6.*

When you have some songs added to iTunes, connect an iPod to your computer using the FireWire or USB 2.0 cable included

Transferring Songs to Your iPod

If this is the first time you're using the iPod with the iTunes software, the transfer of songs should be automatic. As soon as you connect an iPod to your computer, the iTunes software launches, finds the iPod, and uploads your songs. This ease of use is made possible by the Auto-Sync feature, which instantly recognizes an iPod and updates the device with any new songs you've added to iTunes since last connecting with your computer. There is another, manual method for transferring songs, covered in a later chapter, although most users are fine with the Auto-Sync method, because they're not looking for maximum flexibility, but rather maximum ease-of-use.

Note
If you're using the iPod shuffle, you can use the Autofill feature to add a random selection of songs to your device. This feature is great for filling up on songs at the beginning of a day or when leaving on a trip.

Note
The manual method is necessary if you want to connect your iPod to more than one computer, or if you want to utilize some of the more advanced hard drive features of your iPod for managing music and other types of files.

Disconnecting the iPod from Your Computer

After the transfer of music to your iPod is complete, it's time to detach the iPod from your computer. When the *OK to Disconnect* message is displayed in the iTunes status display, it's all right to remove your iPod by ejecting the device. To disconnect your iPod, follow these steps:

1. **Select the iPod device in the iTunes Source list (on the left side of the iTunes application window).**

2. **Click the Eject button next to the device's name.**

3. **Disconnect the cable from your computer and remove your iPod from the Dock connector when the iPod's menu reappears.** If you're using the Dock accessory, you can simply remove the iPod from its cradle. For users of the iPod shuffle, unplug the device from the USB port or special Dock accessory it's connected to.

Playing Songs on Your iPod

Now that you have some songs on your iPod, you can begin to use it in the way it was intended. You may need to get used to the Click Wheel controls (the touch-sensitive controls on the front of your iPod) before going any farther, although they're generally very intuitive and should have you flying through your music collection in no time (unless you're using an iPod shuffle, which has forward and backward controls, but no touch-sensitive wheel).

To navigate the menus, find songs, and play your music, follow these steps:

1. **Scroll with your finger or thumb around the circular track of the Click Wheel controller (moving clockwise or counterclockwise) until you arrive at the Music or Browse option in the main menu.**

2. **Press the center Select button on the Click Wheel to choose the Music or Browse option.**

3. **Use the controller to move to the Artists, Playlists, or Songs option, and choose it by pressing the Select button.**

4. **Scroll up and down the list of available music and find a song you want to play.**

5. **Choose the song by pressing the Select button.**

6. **Pause the song by pressing the Pause/Play button at the bottom of the Click Wheel controls.** To resume playing, press the Pause/Play button once more.

7. **Adjust the volume by sliding your finger around the circular Click Wheel controls.** Moving in a counterclockwise direction lowers the volume, while moving clockwise raises it.

8. **Skip from one song to another by using the Previous and Forward buttons, located on the left and right sides of the Click Wheel controls.**

9. **Return to the main menu by pressing the Menu button a few times.**

10. **When you're ready to turn off your iPod, press and hold the Play/Pause button until it shuts off.** You can turn your iPod back on by pressing the center Select button.

Playing Songs with iPod Shuffle

If you're using an iPod shuffle, the methods for playing songs are a little different from other iPod models, due to the lack of a screen or the same Click Wheel controls. Simply slide the switch on the back of the iPod shuffle to the middle, which is the Play in Order position, if you want all your songs to play back in the same order in which they appear in iTunes. You can also move the switch to the bottom, Shuffle position, which plays back your songs in a random order. Use the Play/Pause button located in the middle of the controls to temporarily pause or resume playback, and the Previous/Rewind button on the left and the Next/Fast-forward button on the right to skip songs. Volume controls are located on the top and bottom of the iPod shuffle controls.

Using the iPod

Exploring the iPod

As you probably read in the introduction, the iPod is a digital music player with the ability to carry thousands of songs, which can be accessed by the swipe of a thumb or the press of a button. An iPod (other than the Shuffle) can also be used as a portable hard drive to hold and transport data, or even as a personal digital assistant (PDA) containing calendar and contact information. As you will learn in this book, there are many uses for an iPod, several of which go beyond the usual use as a portable jukebox. As a device, the iPod continues to evolve, becoming better with each new generation.

Although the iPod's specifications continue to change over time, the basics remain the same. The iPod is about the size of a deck of cards and stores information on a miniature, fixed hard drive. The capacity of its hard drive continues to increase as smaller, more efficient drives become available. For this reason, you may notice that the current 60GB iPod model is actually smaller and thinner than the original 5GB iPod. This evolution toward smaller sizes means the iPod is easier to take with you wherever you go. Whichever model you own, an iPod fits easily in your pocket (in the case of the iPod shuffle, you actually risk losing it in your pocket). Not even the smallest CD or cassette players can make this claim.

Because the iPod is essentially a hard drive with a user-friendly interface, you can use it to carry your entire music collection, along with other computer files, such as photos, Word documents, or the contents of your laptop. Backing up files from work to bring home (or vice versa) is simple with an iPod. You can also use the iPod as a digital organizer or simplified PDA, by using its calendar and address book features.

If you haven't taken advantage of these features yet, you should consider the benefits of using your iPod to stay organized. With your iPod in your pocket, you should never have to miss a meeting again. iPod photo models can also display photos on a special color screen, which is great for on-the-go presentations.

Table 1.1 shows the iPod models that were available for sale when this book was written.

If you already own one of these devices (which is probably the case if you've picked up this book), or if you're looking to invest in an iPod with more features, this chapter will give you just what you need. It introduces you to the main features and specifications of the various iPod models on the market, as well as computer system requirements.

> **Note**
>
> *An in-depth discussion of the features provided by each iPod model is covered more thoroughly in other areas of this book, particularly in regards to using controls, making menu selections, and interfacing with a computer and the iTunes software. Additionally, Apple merged the iPod photo line with their standard iPod device as this book went to press. Therefore, some of the information in this chapter may have changed. For the latest information on iPod devices, visit Apples Web site at* www.apple.com.

iPod Features

The standard iPod that started it all has progressed from a somewhat bulky little box with several buttons to a rather slim case with a single, smooth controller (the latest iPod is also referred to as 4G, after its generation designation). Most iPod owners who have this device use it as their primary music player. Its large capacity makes it attractive, because it can carry a large music collection. But it can also act as a substantial little hard drive for transporting data. Its ability to carry 15,000 songs (or up to 25,000 photos) makes it the iPod of choice for the serious audiophile. Its slick interface, and intuitive Click Wheel design make it easy to learn and use right out of the box.

The iPod's 2-inch color LCD screen (which only recently changed from grayscale) is LED backlit, which means it's bright and doesn't burn out easily from frequent use. iPods have one of the best screens in a device this size and (thanks in part to the backlight feature) make it easy to quickly find a song or album to play, even in a dark room. You might even find yourself using its screen as a flashlight while looking for your keys at night.

Table 1.1
Current iPod Models

iPod Model	Capacity	Average Price
iPod	20GB (5,000 songs) or 60GB (15,000 songs)	$299 or $399
iPod mini	4GB (1,000 songs) or 6GB (1,500 songs)	$199 or $249
iPod U2 Special Edition	20GB (5,000 songs)	$349
iPod shuffle	512MB (120 songs) or 1GB (240 songs)	$99 or $149

Note *Although the number of songs for a 60GB iPod is stated as 15,000, this number is calculated for a four-minute song encoded using AAC compression at a data rate of 128 Kbps, which can vary significantly based on the length of songs or the quality used to import audio tracks. Currently, all songs available in the iTunes Music Store are AAC-encoded at 128 Kbps.*

Depending on when you purchased your device, you may have an older 20GB- or 40GB-capacity iPod with the grayscale screen, or the more recent photo line with color screen in 20GB or 60GB capacities (see the iPod photo section later in this chapter for additional information on color iPods). The available hard drive capacities change over time (and may have been updated by the time you read this).

Note *Remember, even though your entire music collection might fit on a 20GB model with room to spare, you may want to use that extra space on a 60GB drive for transporting data or photos or even as extra room for all those future iTunes Music Store downloads.*

Tip *To save battery life, choose playlists instead of individual tracks. Playlists load more data into the memory at startup, so the hard drive doesn't have to spin as much.*

20GB iPod

Currently, only 20GB and 60GB iPods are available for purchase from Apple. The difference between the 20GB and the 60GB iPod is minimal at best—the obvious difference being the storage space available (and a slimmer case as a result). The smaller unit weighs only 5.9 ounces, considerably less than first-generation devices and only slightly less than the 60GB model. However, the 20GB iPod is still more than enough to hold a large music collection of approximately 5,000 songs. The lack of a Dock accessory (a cradle for easily interfacing with a computer and charging the iPod) in the box means that all connections need to be made directly through the included cables unless you purchase a Dock separately.

Battery Life

Each iPod model has a battery life rated at 12 hours or more (15 hours for current color models), although actual times will vary depending on usage. Frequent use of the backlight feature, for example, drains a significant amount of power. You might also see your battery's ability to hold a charge diminish over time (usually after a year or so), which is to be expected from a rechargeable lithium ion battery. Fortunately, Apple now offers a program for relatively inexpensive battery replacement (under $100), although an unofficial method is also discussed later in this book. Your battery can be fully charged in four hours and a fast charge can be reached in about two hours, which brings the battery to 80 percent capacity when you need to charge on the run.

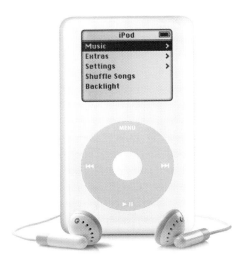

1.1 The iPod comes in 20GB and 60GB capacities.

Tip *Although the previous iPod's display is black-and-white (with a bluish tint when using the backlight), you can find companies online that mod (modify) your screen's color by switching out the color of the LED light (to make it red or green, for example). Keep in mind that making any modifications to an iPod, or even opening its case, may void your warranty.*

Each iPod is designed with a Dock connector on the bottom, instead of the old FireWire port on the top, which began on the original iPod. Using a special Dock connector makes it possible for the iPod to be slimmer, while still allowing the cable to break out to a FireWire or USB 2.0 connector at the other end.

40GB iPod

In a previous reshuffling of its iPod lineup, Apple discontinued a 40GB iPod model, choosing instead to focus on its series of iPod photo devices. And, in fact, now all iPods have color screens and are photo capable, and the iPod photo moniker has been eliminated.

At 6.2 ounces the 40GB iPod was only slightly heavier and thicker than the 20GB model. At twice the capacity, it could hold approximately 10,000 songs, although the

1.2 Apart from capacity, the only difference between the older 20GB and 40GB iPods was the addition of a Dock accessory with the larger unit, although the Dock must still be purchased separately for use with the 20GB and 60GB models.

extra space might be best utilized as a hard drive for transporting data files. All other specifications and menu options remain the same, with the exception of accessories. The 40GB iPod came with a Dock, without connecting and disconnecting cables. You might also decide to purchase a special iPod "boom box" (like those sold by Bose, JBL, and Altec Lansing), which adds speakers to your iPod and charges it at the same time.

iPod controls

In addition to the Click Wheel controls — which include forward, backward, menu, play/pause, and select command options, as well as volume control by sliding your finder around the wheel — each iPod is equipped with a Hold switch on the top of the device. When activated, the Hold switch prevents buttons from being accidentally pushed while in your pocket. It also makes sure that you can begin from where you left off listening, without mistakenly changing any settings or skipping to another track.

Next to the Hold switch on the top of the iPod is the iPod Remote port (for attaching an optional remote control) and the Headphones port. The ability to use a remote control is a nice feature, since you may often find yourself placing the iPod in a coat pocket, where locating the right buttons

to press sometimes requires a bit of guesswork. With a remote control together with your headphone cord, you can more readily switch tracks, fast-forward, or pause playback. Still, with the newer Click Wheel design, finding the right controls without looking takes a minimum of practice for many users.

iPod case

Apart from the iPod controls and technical specifications, the case is a sometimes overlooked feature of the iPod. The iPod case is sturdy and seamless, making it comfortable to hold (and easy on the eyes). You may have already discovered that the case, which has a chrome-like finish on the back, is also rather easy to mark with fingerprints. While a soft cloth can remove surface smudges, a good case is an option to consider if you're concerned about protecting your iPod investment from permanent scarring. Protective cases and jackets not only provide a way to prevent scratches and marks on the iPod's casing and screen, they can also help to prevent the iPod case from cracking when an iPod is accidentally dropped, or when pressure is applied to them while lying in the bottom of a bag. A wide variety of iPod cases are available, although hard shell designs are usually the best if you want to avoid damage.

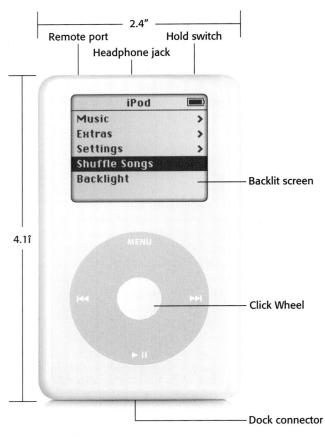

Courtesy of Apple
1.3 iPod controls include the Click Wheel design for navigating menus and selecting songs.

iPod Mini Features

The iPod mini is Apple's answer to micro MP3 players (mostly flash RAM devices) that have been available for a few years. Although the iPod mini's storage capacity is comparatively small at 4GB or 6GB, it's perfect for users who are more concerned with portability and less concerned with the need to carry their entire music collection with them everywhere. It's ideal for athletic activities, such as jogging and snowboarding, thanks to its small size, the availability of armbands, optional watertight housings, and 25 minutes of skip protection (the same as standard iPods). Since it is about the size of a credit card and weighs only 3.6 ounces, the iPod mini is equally desirable for those fashion-conscious users who want to minimize the "footprint" of digital devices they carry. A range of four colors to choose from adds to its appeal. Although it's significantly smaller than the standard 4G iPod model, it is virtually the same device, and many of the same features and considerations apply.

The iPod mini uses the same controls as the larger 4G iPod. The Click Wheel design, which makes navigating so simple and fun in its precursor, was actually developed first for the iPod mini — the lack of space on a device this small made the inclusion of extra buttons (as seen on earlier iPod models) difficult to include. The Hold switch, iPod Remote port, and Headphones port also remain the same, as does a Dock connector port, which is now standard on all iPod devices (iPod shuffle is the exception). It does not come with a Dock, although you can purchase a Dock separately if you do not already own one. It also ships with a belt clip, which is perfect for taking with you on the treadmill at the gym.

Due to its compact size, an iPod mini's battery is rated at 18 hours, versus the 12 hours for the standard iPod model. The full charge time remains the same (at 4 hours), as well as the fast charge time, which is listed at 2 hours to achieve 80 percent capacity. Its smaller, 1.67-inch screen is nearly as easy to read as the screen on the 4G iPod, and its menu system remains the same.

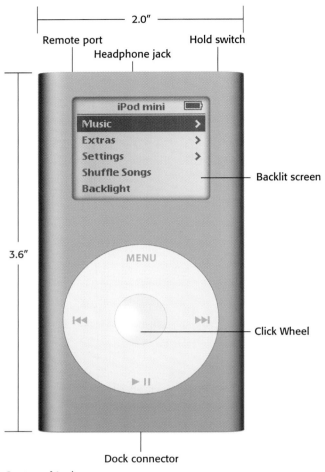

Remote port

Headphone jack

Hold switch

2.0"

3.6"

iPod mini

Music >
Extras >
Settings >
Shuffle Songs
Backlight

Backlit screen

MENU

Click Wheel

Dock connector

Courtesy of Apple

1.4 At only 3.6 ounces, and smaller than most cell phones, the iPod mini is small enough to take anywhere.

Courtesy of Apple
1.5 The iPod mini comes in a selection of four colors.

iPod Photo Features

It was only a matter of time before Apple decided to join the fray of portable digital devices that did more than carry music or act as a miniature hard drive. In its biggest step forward to date, the iPod lineup is now joined by iPod photo, a device that permits the storage and viewing of digital photos and album art in addition to songs. iPod photo is available in 30GB and 60GB capacities, enough for 7,500 or 15,000 songs, respectively. Its integration with iPhoto software mirrors the iPod's relationship with iTunes, further expanding the usefulness of the iLife suite of applications. Despite its added photo functionality and color screen, many of the same features from the 4G iPods are present in this device, including the touch-sensitive Click Wheel design, Dock Connector, and Hold switch, as well as an iPod Remote port (which doubles as an AV port for slideshow presentations) and a Headphones port.

Exchanging the black-and-white LCD screen found in the standard, mini, and Special Edition iPods with a vibrant 65,536 color screen, iPod photo represents one of the best ways to view images on the go. It's a handy device for digital photographers in the field, who can use a photo reader adapter (such as the accessory sold by Apple or those made by Belkin) to upload and view their pictures. It's also a great portable presentation device that can be hooked up to a television or projector for giving simple presentations. As a sign of things to come, Kodak recently announced that it will stop producing slide projectors, which years ago were one of the primary ways to watch images from family vacations in living rooms across the world. Although iPod photo does not deliver quality better than a 35mm slide projector, it can be used to easily display images on that most ubiquitous of household devices — the television. Better still, an iPod photo can carry up to 25,000 photos wherever you go (if no music is included), which can be viewed on a plane, on a train, in a boardroom, in a classroom, or anywhere else you might find yourself.

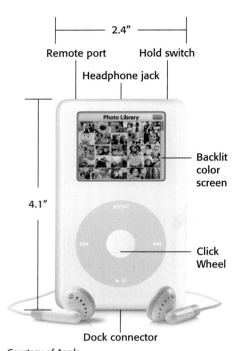

2.4″

Remote port   Hold switch

Headphone jack

Photo Library

Backlit color screen

4.1″

MENU

Click Wheel

Dock connector

Courtesy of Apple

1.6 The iPod photo was the first iPod to offer a color screen and the ability to view images.

If you haven't discovered it already, one of the great features of iPod photo is the ability to automatically generate a slideshow with smooth transitions and a musical soundtrack. This is great for showing off pictures from your latest trip to friends at school, or images of your kids and pets to anyone you might meet on the street. For digital artists, it's a great way to quickly present your portfolio when you run into a potential employer at the coffeehouse down the block.

Even simple games, such as solitaire, look better when rendered in full color (a few games come standard on all iPod models with a screen). Calendar functions also look better somehow when selected days of the week are highlighted in blue or when a battery power icon is shown in a vibrant green. Also, album covers that you've stored with your music become viewable as you listen to a particular song.

The iPod photo comes with the usual accessories, including earphones, AC adapter, and FireWire/USB 2.0 cables. It also ships with a special iPod photo AV cable and iPod photo Dock, for connecting to a television or other display device.

iPod U2 Special Edition Features

The iPod U2 Special Edition is essentially the same device as the standard 20GB fourth-generation iPod discussed earlier, with a few cosmetic differences. The only alterations are the case color, which is black with a red Click Wheel, the laser-engraved names of members from U2 on the back, and the option to download "The Complete U2" box set from the iTunes Music Store at a $50 discount (it includes 446 songs and 40 rare and unreleased tracks).

Courtesy of Apple

1.7 The iPod U2 Special Edition model.

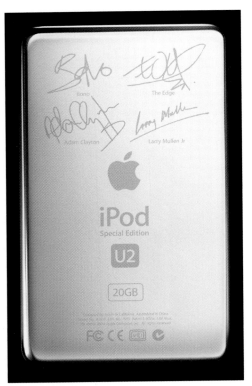

1.8 The autographs of U2 band members are etched on the back of the iPod U2 Special Edition.

iPod Shuffle Features

iPod shuffle is the latest incarnation of Apple's popular music player—and also the smallest. The diminutive size of the iPod shuffle, which is comparable to a pack of gum, makes it perfect for taking everywhere. You can use it as you would any other iPod. The iPod shuffle is perfect for high-impact sports, because it's a flash-based device, not employing a hard drive like the other iPods. The use of non-movable, flash-based memory means it doesn't skip the way a spinning hard drive mechanism or a CD player can. However, even the iPod shuffle is susceptible to hard impacts. To make it fit better into your exercise routine, you can augment your iPod shuffle with a variety of accessories, such as an armband or sport case (in addition to the *lanyard,* or cord, that came with your device).

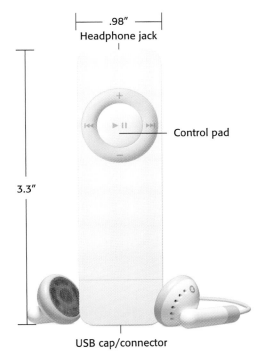

.98"

Headphone jack

Control pad

3.3"

USB cap/connector

Courtesy of Apple

1.9 The compact iPod shuffle, Apple's latest digital music player, has controls that make it easy to navigate without the use of a screen.

The iPod shuffle is currently available in two capacities: 512MB and 1GB. The 512MB model holds at most about 120 songs, while the 1GB device can hold about 240 songs. Both models hold significantly less than their full-sized, iPod counterparts, but this is still enough space for about 8–16 hours of music. So, it's great for day-to-day use, short trips, and high-energy activities.

The iPod shuffle's size makes it impractical for a screen to view songs and playlists, like those used on other iPod models. For this reason, you need to rely solely on circular playback controls on the front of the device and a special switch on the back. (Apple's decision to forgo the screen was a wise move, as it cuts down on the cost of the device, and makes its operation more practical and streamlined.) The controls on the front of the iPod shuffle allow you to easily skip tracks, pause a song, or turn the volume up and down. Although it does not use the standard Click Wheel controls (with a touch-sensitive ring for adjusting volume and navigating menus), if you've used any of the other iPod models, this type of operation should feel natural. Even if it's your first time using the iPod shuffle, the controls should be easy to use.

The popular shuffle feature, which many users already rely on with their other iPod models, is the primary method for controlling playback (hence its name). You can activate the shuffle feature by flipping the slider on the back of the iPod shuffle, which randomly selects a song for you to listen to. In this way, you never know what song to expect next, which is a great choice for the indecisive or adventurous listener. Of course, you can also choose to play back songs in order, for when you want to listen to a particular album or playlist (or an audiobook). When loading up your iPod shuffle with new songs, the Autofill function can be used to randomly select music for a new playlist. In this way, every time you leave for work in the morning, you can quickly take a new batch of randomly selected music with you for the commute.

Like the other iPod models, iPod shuffle can be charged by attaching it directly to your computer or through the use of a separately connected Dock. The main difference between this device and other iPods is that the iPod shuffle can connect directly to your computer through the USB port (no FireWire option), without the use of a cable. You may

iPod Hard Drives versus Flash RAM

Because iPods consist of a hard drive mechanism for storing music and data, they aren't limited by the size of removable disk media, which means that iPods can become smaller and thinner as storage technology improves. However, for very small devices, flash RAM (or miniature, non-moveable memory cards) is actually more practical and efficient. RAM is also more expensive than traditional hard drive mechanisms and currently too costly for storing large amounts of data. At the present time, the only iPod model to employ flash RAM is the iPod shuffle, which comes in relatively small 512MB and 1GB capacities. In the future, more iPod devices may use flash RAM, such as a proposed Motorola phone with the ability to play iTunes music.

Apart from their smaller size, flash RAM devices are not susceptible to the skipping that occurs from sudden movements or impacts that affect spinning hard drive mechanisms. This is why the iPod shuffle is great for exercise and sport enthusiasts. Nonetheless, most iPod models are equipped with a 25-minute skip protection feature (the iPod photo's skip protection is up to 17 minutes), which temporarily stores song information — using a type of RAM — for retrieval in case of shocks. This feature makes it possible to jog or engage in other physical activities with an iPod.

already be familiar with this type of connectivity if you use a flash memory device to transport data from one computer to another. In fact, the iPod shuffle can be used to hold data as well as songs. This means that you can listen to music on the way to work, while carrying your PowerPoint presentation on the same device. If you find yourself away from a computer for an extended period of time, you might consider purchasing the optional USB power adapter, which lets you plug the iPod shuffle into an electrical outlet. There is also an optional battery pack that operates on two AAA batteries, which can be connected to the iPod shuffle for an additional 20 hours of music enjoyment.

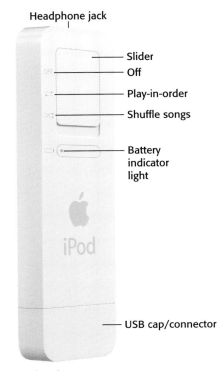

Headphone jack

Slider

Off

Play-in-order

Shuffle songs

Battery indicator light

iPod

USB cap/connector

Courtesy of Apple

1.10 A switch on the back of the iPod shuffle allows you to choose between shuffle and play-in-order modes, which changes the way you listen to your music.

System Requirements

Regardless of which iPod model you own, there are certain minimum requirements that your home computer must meet in order to work with the device. These requirements differ from Macs to PCs, and occasionally from one iPod model to another. In general, using an iPod doesn't require a fast or expensive computer, but it does require that you're up to date on the latest software. A relatively recent operating system doesn't hurt either. Fortunately, the iTunes software that is used together with an iPod is free for both Macs and PCs. In addition, an Internet connection is recommended if you want to take advantage of the iTunes Music Store or retrieve CD content information, but it isn't necessary. Make certain to check out the requirements for your platform of choice before trying to use your iPod.

Macintosh system requirements

If you're a Mac user, you should be running a version of OS X that is at least 10.1.5 or later. OS X 10.4 and above is ideal, particularly for use with some of the newer iPod models with photo and podcast features. The iPod shuffle requires at least Mac OS X 10.2.8 or 10.3.4, while 10.1.5 is possible (but not recommended) for the standard iPod model.

Updates to iPod and iTunes software are posted periodically, although checking online news groups to see if any problems have been reported with the software is usually a good idea. (You're usually fine downloading these updates right away.) If you have Software Update activated on a

Mac, you should be notified when a new version becomes available and prompted to install the software. You can also check the Support section on the Apple site for more information (www.apple.com/support) regarding new downloads.

Tip

For the latest system requirements for your particular iPod, make sure to check the Apple site at www.apple.com/ itunes *and click on your iPod model at the top of the screen.*

Apart from the necessary software to use your iPod, it's important that your Mac is equipped with at least one FireWire port (the ideal connection, for the fastest transfer speeds) or one USB 2.0 port located on the computer. A USB port on a keyboard or other peripheral might not be powered, and as a result, insufficient for charging capabilities to your iPod. Because all recent Macs (even those from several years ago) are equipped with one or more of these connections, this isn't a problem for the majority of users. A minimum of 256MB of RAM and a 400 MHz or faster processor is necessary to work with an iPod, although faster machines are usually recommended.

Courtesy of Apple

1.11 An ideal Mac setup might include a 17-inch or 20-inch iMac, which comes with the iLife suite of applications with iTunes already installed.

Windows system requirements

If you're using your iPod with a PC, it's important that you make certain you've purchased a PC version of the device, or that you're willing to reformat your iPod drive from a Mac-only device to a PC-compatible hard drive format. Fortunately, the latest version of Windows XP can still recognize a Mac-formatted iPod when it's connected to a PC, although it should prompt you to reformat the drive as a FAT32 volume. A Macintosh computer can read these PC-formatted drives, although any data that was on the drive is erased in the reformatting process.

Note *Although Macintosh hard drives (an iPod is essentially a hard drive that can also play music) are formatted as Mac OS extended volumes, PCs don't work with Mac-formatted drives and require a FAT32 volume instead.*

A few different PC operating systems are supported for use with an iPod. These include Windows 2000 (with Service Pack 4 installed), Windows XP Home, or Windows XP Professional. As with Macs, PCs require a FireWire or USB 2.0 port for connecting to the iPod, either directly or through the iPod Dock Connector. Most PCs sold in the last few years are easily capable of working with an iPod. As long as your computer has 256MB of RAM and a 500 MHz or faster processor you should be fine.

Setting Up
the iPod

I f you're a new iPod user, particularly if you're from the PC world, initially you might be surprised at how easy it is to navigate and use the controls and settings on your iPod. In fact, you may already have a grasp on these topics shortly after opening the box. Regardless how user-friendly the iPods are, you are bound to have a few questions about your controls and the available settings. This chapter addresses these topics and provides some details pertaining to specific iPod models.

Using iPod Controls

iPod controls are easy and intuitive, thanks to the Apple Click Wheel design that is a part of the entire iPod family (although the new iPod shuffle is a little different). The Click Wheel is touch-sensitive and allows you to navigate all the menus without lifting your thumb from the device. Simply slide your thumb around the wheel and click on the various options (Menu, Next arrow, Back arrow, Play/Pause) to move through the menu choices, or press the center Select button to make a selection. To go back to a previous menu page, repeatedly click the Menu option at the top of the Click Wheel, backtracking through the menu screens until you arrive at the desired menu, similar to a Web browser's Back button operation.

In addition to using the Click Wheel to navigate your iPod by scrolling up and down through lists of songs and menu options, you can slide your thumb (much like sliding your finger on a laptop computer's trackpad to move the cursor) counterclockwise to lower the volume or clockwise to raise it as songs are playing. This type of control applies to all the iPod models, except the iPod shuffle. To adjust the volume on

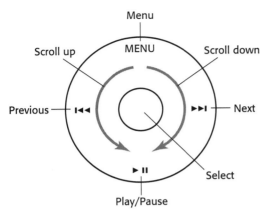

2.1 The iPod Click Wheel design makes menu navigation easy.

an iPod shuffle, you need to physically press the + or - at the top and bottom of the wheel. Skipping tracks is simply a matter of pressing the forward arrow or the backward arrow on the front of the iPod shuffle, which may remind some users of the older-generation iPod models, particularly the first iPod design.

Another control feature on all iPods (except the iPod shuffle) is a Hold switch. The Hold feature prevents you from accidentally activating a button while carrying your iPod in a pocket. Simply slide the switch until you see an orange bar, which indicates that the iPod controls are locked off from being used until you slide the Hold switch back again.

Note *Being the middle child of the iPod family, the iPod mini is sometimes forgotten while discussing features of the other devices. Fortunately, the iPod mini shares the same controls and menu options with its larger siblings. If you already know how to use a standard iPod, the iPod mini is the same, only smaller. The iPod shuffle, on the other hand, is the youngest and simplest of the iPod line. Its basic design, which uses stripped-down navigation and lacks a screen for making adjustments and menu selections, is perfect for letting the music take control.*

2.2 The Hold switch prevents accidentally pressing a button while carrying an iPod in a pocket or bag.

Adjusting iPod Settings

Several possible settings and menu options are available for you to use to customize your iPod experience. If you've already begun playing with your iPod, you should have noticed the variety of menus and sub-menu options to choose from. This section includes a few of the initial choices you might make when first setting up your iPod and learning to use the controls.

Setting the backlight timer

The backlight is an extremely useful option for helping you to read the iPod display in poor lighting conditions. It also looks really nice when it lights up, which makes it great for showing off a new iPod to friends. The only drawback to using the backlight is that it can significantly drain your battery if used too much. Although you can turn on the backlight easily from the main menu by simply clicking Backlight, you may want to set the duration of the backlight (the amount of time the screen remains lit) by adjusting the timer setting. Typically, a backlight timer doesn't require a long duration, because it remains lit as long as you're touching the controls. If a backlight is necessary, a timer of 2 or 5 seconds is enough for most users and cuts down on power consumption. Of course, the best way to conserve power is to not use a backlight at all. However, for low-light or no-light situations, it's a great feature to have.

Follow these steps to adjust the backlight timer:

1. **From the iPod main menu, select Settings ⇨ Backlight Timer.** A new menu page appears.

2. **Scroll down this new menu page until you see the Backlight Timer option, and click the Select button.**

3. **Choose a duration.** Choices range from 2 Seconds to 20 Seconds, or you can decide to keep the backlight Always On or Always Off. Remember that the longer your backlight remains on, the faster your battery will become depleted during heavy use.

4. **Click the Menu button to return to the main menu.**

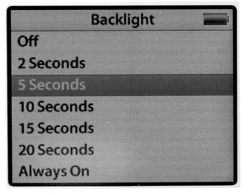

2.3 Backlight menu settings.

Adjusting screen contrast

In addition to the availability of a backlight for reading in dark places, you can control contrast (for iPods with black and white screens) to improve the legibility of text in bright environments or when viewing at different angles. Although you may never need to change the default setting, which places contrast in the middle of the range, you can follow these steps at any time to increase or decrease contrast of the display.

1. **From the iPod main menu, select Settings ➪ Contrast.** The contrast setting screen appears.

2. **Move your thumb clockwise around the Click Wheel to increase contrast and counterclockwise to decrease Contrast.** You will see the bar on the screen fill and empty as you increase and decrease the contrast.

3. **When you're finished making your adjustment, click the Menu button twice to return to the main menu.**

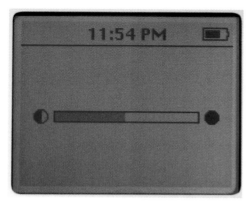

2.4 Contrast menu setting.

Setting date and time

Although it isn't crucial, keeping your iPod current by setting the correct date and time is a good idea. This setting is probably the second one most users make, after choosing the correct language, when starting up an iPod for the first time.

Follow these steps to set the date and time for your iPod:

1. **From the iPod main menu, select Settings ➪ Date & Time.** A new menu screen appears with options for date and time.

2. **Select Set Time Zone and choose the appropriate area, such as US Eastern (DST).** DST stands for daylight saving time.

3. **In the Date & Time menu, select Set Date & Time.**

4. **Use the Click Wheel to increase or decrease the highlighted number, and then click to advance to the next set of numbers.** Return to the previous menu by clicking the Menu button when you've made your final selection here.

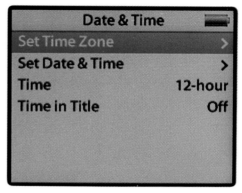

2.5 Date and Time menu settings.

Choosing a new language

The first time you use an iPod and click a button to wake it up, you're presented with a choice of 14 different display languages. At any time in the future, you can go back into a settings menu and switch to another display language. Your choice of language only affects Apple menu options and character sets that are capable of being displayed; it doesn't translate song titles and other information into another language.

If for some reason you decide to change the language, follow these steps:

1. **Select Settings from the iPod main menu.** The Settings menu screen appears.

2. **Scroll all the way to the bottom of this screen and select Language.** A list of available languages appears.

3. **Choose the appropriate display language from the list of 14 available options.** Choices include English, Finnish, Japanese, German, Spanish, French, Italian, and several others.

4. **Return to any higher-level menu by clicking the Menu button until the desired menu is displayed.**

Changing the Clicker

You may have already noticed that the iPod provides the option to hear an audible clicking sound as you navigate the menus. This sound, which provides feedback that you may or may not like, can be turned on or off at any time. It can also be made audible with or without headphones attached. By default, the Clicker is turned on, so you may want to adjust this setting before proceeding much farther with your iPod. The Clicker can be a nuisance or embarrassment if you're caught using your iPod in a public location, such as a lecture hall, library, or other quiet space.

The following steps demonstrate how to turn the Clicker on and off:

1. **Select Settings from the iPod main menu.** The Settings menu screen appears.

2. **Scroll down the new page and select Clicker.**

2.6 Language menu settings.

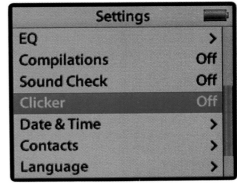

2.7 Clicker menu settings.

3. **Press the center button to change the options.** When you find the option you want, click Menu to return to the main menu. Choices include Headphones (for hearing the Clicker sound only when headphones are attached), Speaker, Both, or Off.

Finding About information

At any time while using your iPod, you may check how many songs you currently have stored, as well as how much space (capacity) you have available on the hard drive. You can also check to see that you have the latest version of the iPod software installed or even check the serial or model number of your device, in case you need to provide it to a service agent when requesting repairs.

Follow these steps to find information about your iPod:

1. **From the iPod main menu, select Settings.** The Settings menu appears.

2. **Scroll to the top of the Settings menu and select About.**

About

Chad Fahs's iPod Photo

Songs	1562
Photos	0
Capacity	55.8 GB
Available	49.4 GB
Version	1.2
S/N	

2.8 The About screen provides information about your iPod.

3. **When you're finished viewing About information for your iPod, click Menu until you return to the main menu.**

Viewing legal information

If you're interested in viewing the legal information that Apple provides about the names and technologies licensed for use in the iPod, you can select the Legal option in the main Settings menu. Most users aren't interested in this little feature, but it can be fun to take a look if you want to practice navigating text documents using the Click Wheel.

Take the following steps to view the iPod's legal copy and practice using the Click Wheel for scrolling through text documents:

1. **In the main menu, select Settings.**

2. **Scroll down the Settings menu page and select Legal.**

3. **Use the Click Wheel to scroll up and down the page and read the text that appears.** Scrolling through long text documents requires you to rotate your thumb around the Click Wheel more than usual.

4. **Press the Menu button twice to return to the main menu.**

Charging the battery and connecting with the Dock

The first thing any new iPod user must do is to make certain that the device is charged. (It should come with a little power already for initial setup operations, so it's all right if you don't have immediate access to a computer or wall outlet.) Every iPod model (other than the iPod shuffle) comes with an AC adapter and a special FireWire cable (one end is a 6-pin FireWire cable, the other is an iPod Dock Connector), which together can be used to directly draw power from the wall and charge your iPod. If your computer has a powered USB 2.0 port, the included iPod Dock Connector to USB 2.0 cable can be used instead. In addition, the iPod is able to draw power through a FireWire cable that is attached to a computer, allowing you to charge an iPod and work with organizing and transferring music at the same time.

Although you can connect the FireWire or USB 2.0 cable from your iPod directly to a desktop or laptop computer, the Dock accessory makes it easier to charge a battery and transfer data, because you only need to drop an iPod into its cradle — no wires to connect or disconnect. Current iPods do not come with a Dock, although you can purchase one separately. Attach the FireWire or USB 2.0 cable to the Dock in place of the iPod. Attaching the iPod to charge the

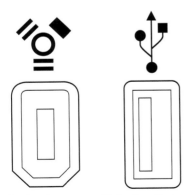

2.9 The iPod comes with both a 6-pin FireWire 400 connector (on the left) and a USB 2.0 connector (on the right) with an iPod Dock Connector at the opposite end.

battery is a simple process after the Dock is assembled and your computer is turned on. Simply rest the iPod in the cradle and let it recharge while you manage your music.

Setting Up iPod Photo

The procedures for setting up an iPod photo are similar to the standard, 4G iPods, which I covered briefly in the Quick Tour chapter at the beginning of this book (these include the U2 Special Edition and the iPod mini). In general, the only difference is the iPod photo's colorful menu screens. However, a few new features set the iPod photo apart from other members of the iPod family. For this reason, considering the iPod photo's unique personality by taking a look at its biggest additions is necessary.

Viewing album artwork

As you play songs on your iPod photo, you may choose to display album artwork associated with that track on the iPod photo's color display. This is one of the features, apart from the viewing of photos, that makes the iPod photo different from other iPod models. For every song or album you download off the iTunes Music Store, or for albums that you've scanned or in which you've downloaded your own images, you can see a thumbnail graphic to accompany the artist and track name on your screen.

 For more about using the iTunes Music Store, see Chapter 5.

To look at album artwork for a song you're playing on your iPod photo, you must first set up iTunes to allow your iPod photo to display album artwork by using the iTunes application and the appropriate option menu.

Note *If you've worked through the Quick Tour at the beginning of this book, you've already had a short preview of the iTunes application.*

Follow these steps to view album artwork:

1. **Attach iPod photo to your computer and open the iTunes application (if it doesn't open automatically) by clicking its icon in the Dock on a Mac.** You can also choose its name from Start ➪ All Programs on a PC.

iTunes

2.10 Open the iTunes application.

2.

  With iPod Photo attached to your computer, click the iPod Photo device in the iTunes Source list. Before you make any changes to the device, it must be selected.

3. **Click the Options icon in the bottom-right corner of the iTunes application window to open the iTunes preferences window, displaying the iPod Options pane.**

2.11 The Options menu for your iPod is accessed through a button in the lower-right corner of the iTunes window.

4. **Make sure the Display Album Artwork on Your iPod option is checked.**

5. **Test the settings you make by playing a song that has artwork associated with it.**

6. **Press the iPod's Select button to see the artwork automatically displayed on the iPod photo screen.**

Although the ability to view album artwork is a nice extra feature to have, the primary usefulness of the iPod photo device is the storage and display of digital photos.

Transferring photos to iPod photo

If you have some images or photos on your computer, you can transfer them easily to iPod photo for viewing on its built-in screen or on a separate television or monitor. There are a few different ways to transfer photos from your computer to an iPod photo. The first two methods, which are perhaps the simplest way to work, involve using iPhoto (on a Mac) and Adobe Photoshop Elements or Photoshop Album on a PC to synchronize your photos — much like synchronizing your music files on other iPods using iTunes.

Transferring from Mac

If you own a Mac, use the following method to transfer images to your iPod photo.

Note *iPhoto 4.0.3 or later is required for automatically transferring photos from a Mac.*

1. **Attach iPod photo to your computer and open the iTunes application (if it doesn't open automatically) by clicking its icon in the Dock.** You must set up iPod photo through iTunes, just as you would any other iPod device.

2. **Select your iPod photo from the source list on the left side of the main iTunes window.**

3. **Click the Options button for your iPod in the lower-right corner of the iTunes interface.** The iTunes preferences window appears with the iPod Options pane selected.

4. **Select the Photos pane.**

5. **In the Photos pane, select the Synchronize photos from option, and then choose iPhoto from the pop-up menu.**

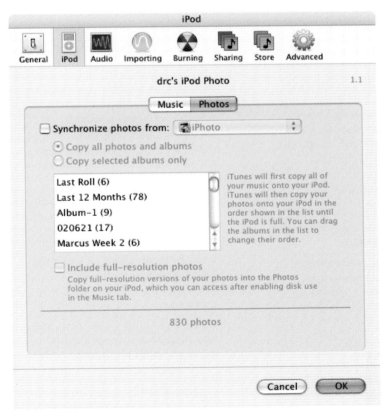

2.12 The iPod Photos pane.

6. **Select the Copy All Photos and Albums radio button if you want all the photos in your iPhoto library, as well as all albums (iPhoto albums are similar to playlists in iTunes), to be copied over to your iPod photo.** You may also choose Copy Selected Albums Only to select individual collections of photos to copy over from the list box.

Transferring from Windows

If you own a PC, use the following method to transfer images to your iPod Photo:

 Note *Minimum requirements for automatically transferring your photos on a PC are Adobe Photoshop Elements 3.0 or Adobe Photoshop Album 1.0.*

1. **Attach iPod photo to your computer and open the iTunes application (if it doesn't open automatically) by choosing its name from Start ⇨ All Programs.** You must set up iPod photo through iTunes, just as you would for any other iPod device.

2. **Select your iPod photo from the source list on the left side of the main iTunes window.**

3. **Click the Options button for your iPod in the lower-right corner of the iTunes interface.** The iPod Options pane of iTunes Preferences appears.

4. **Select the Photos tab.**

5. **Choose Synchronize Photos From and select Photoshop Elements or Photoshop Album from the pop-up menu.**

6. **Choose Copy All Photos and Albums if you want use all the photos in your Photoshop Elements or Photoshop Album collections.** You may also choose Copy Selected Albums Only to choose individual collections of photos to copy over.

In addition to using an application (iPhoto, Photoshop Elements 3, or Photoshop Album) to synchronize your photos, you can transfer photos manually by copying files from your hard drive onto an iPod photo as data.

Manually copying for Mac or Windows

If you don't want to have your computer automatically copy over all of your photos, follow these steps:

1. **Arrange the images you want to copy over to your iPod photo in a folder on your computer.** You can create subfolders inside a main folder if you want your images to appear as separate albums within iPod photo.

2. **Attach iPod photo to your computer and open the iTunes application (if it doesn't open automatically) by clicking its Dock icon on a Mac or choosing its name from Start ⇨ All Programs on a Windows machine.**

3. **Select your iPod photo from the Source list on the left side of the main iTunes window.**

4. **Click the Options button for your iPod in the lower-right corner of the iTunes interface.**

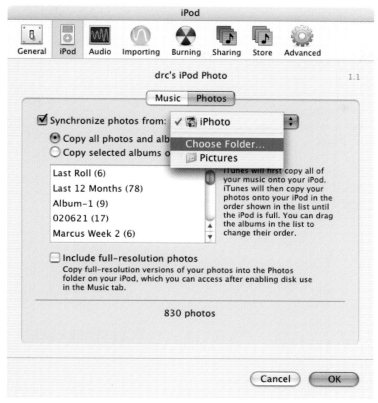

2.13 Choosing an option from the Synchronize photos from drop-down list.

5. **Select the Photos tab.**

6. **Select the Synchronize photos from option.**

7. **Select Choose Folder from the Synchronize photos from drop-down list.** An Open dialog box appears.

8. **Locate the folder on your hard drive with the images you want to transfer to your iPod photo, select it, and click Choose.** iTunes will now proceed to transfer the images in the selected folder to your iPod photo.

Tip

If you want to transfer full-resolution photos to your iPod photo, select the Include Full-Resolution Photos option from the Photo tab during Step 5 in the preceding set of steps. Usually, photos are automatically optimized for viewing on iPod photo before transferring, in order to save space and view more easily.

Connecting iPod photo to a television

iPod photo differs from the other iPod models in the way its special Dock accessory can connect to a TV for presenting slideshow images. Using either a standard S-video cable or a special AV cable, which carries both video and audio information, you can display your photos on any suitably equipped video device. Connect your iPod photo using the supplied cables and make sure that your Slideshow Settings menu option for TV Out is set to Ask or On (main iPod menu ⇨ Photos ⇨ Slideshow Settings ⇨ TV Out). If the Ask option is selected, each time a slideshow is activated iPod photo will prompt you to choose whether you want to view it on the built-in screen or an a separately connected television. Setting the TV Out option to On means that all slideshows are automatically sent out through the AV cables and special Dock accessory. Also, make sure to select the appropriate TV standard (NTSC or PAL) if it isn't already selected from your Slideshow Settings menu.

iPod Basics and More

O nce you've made a few basic settings to set up your iPod, as described in Chapter 2, it's time to learn how to connect your iPod to a computer, transfer music, and use a few of its more specialized features. In this chapter, the basics of iPod usage are covered and expanded upon. Later chapters cover some associated topics in greater detail, particularly those related to the use of the iPod as a hard drive for storing data and the implications of using its notes feature for reading books and viewing e-mail.

Connecting and Disconnecting an iPod

In order to transfer music and files from your computer to an iPod (and vice versa), you need to first connect the device using a FireWire cable or USB 2.0 cable, which are provided with all new iPods (except the iPod shuffle, which connects directly through an empty USB port, or a special Dock accessory). You may also have a Dock connected to your computer, using one of these cables. In this case, you can simply place your iPod in the cradle to automatically connect with your computer. Once your iPod is connected using one of these methods, iTunes automatically launches and your computer treats the iPod as if it were a hard drive device (whether it shows up as a traditional hard drive volume depends on the settings you have made in iTunes). And, your iPod really is a hard drive — it can be used to store data and files.

To disconnect an iPod from your computer, first make certain it isn't in the process of updating files (a message appears saying "Do not disconnect" if it is). Disconnecting an iPod while it's in use can cause damage to the files that are being transferred. When you're ready to remove the device, click the Eject button next to the iPod's icon in the iTunes Source list (located on the left side of the screen, along with your playlists), or select the device in the Source list and click the Eject button located in the lower-right corner of the iTunes window. If you're working on a Mac, you can also drag the iPod icon from the desktop into the Trash, which ejects the iPod like any other device. On a PC, you can eject your iPod by clicking the

Safely Remove Hardware icon in the System Tray (located in the lower-right corner of your screen) and selecting the iPod device to remove. Once your iPod has been ejected, you can disconnect it by lifting it from the Dock or disconnecting the FireWire or USB 2.0 cable.

Note When an iPod is connected to your computer, it automatically draws power to charge its battery. If you're connecting to a non-powered FireWire or USB port on your computer, you may need a special device for supplying external power, such the FireWire cables sold by Sik (www.sik.com).

Eject button

3.1 The Eject button in iTunes unmounts an iPod from your computer, allowing you to safely disconnect the device.

Transferring Songs and Playlists to an iPod

An iPod is only as good as the songs (or images and other files) you have on it. Before you can appreciate what an iPod has to offer, you need to import some music from a CD or download some music files from the iTunes Music Store (as we discuss in a later chapter). The iTunes software adds these songs to your library and allows you to manage your music using *playlists,* which are queues of songs that play back in a predefined order. In order to transfer these songs and playlists to your iPod, you first need to connect it to your computer, as described in the preceding section. Once a connection is established, you have two basic options for transferring songs to the device.

Adding songs and playlists with Auto-Sync

The first option for transferring music is to have iTunes automatically update the songs and playlists on your iPod, which requires no additional steps on your part. This is the Auto-Sync feature that Apple often refers to in its advertising and list of important iPod features, which keeps track of new songs and playlists added to your iTunes software and automatically mirrors your iPod to match.

Auto-Sync is the method you'll probably use, because it's the simplest, no-hassle process for getting new music onto your iPod. It makes transferring songs and playlists to an iPod simple and painless, but while sacrificing the flexibility to, for example, include songs on your iPod that you don't have in your iTunes Library.

Given the widespread acceptance and usage of iPods, there are also many users who aren't as computer savvy as multimedia aficionados and hardcore iPod fanatics (I use the term affectionately). Because this is the default operation for iTunes and an iPod, you shouldn't have to do anything to activate the Auto-Sync feature. However, if iTunes doesn't launch automatically and update your iPod with the new songs in your library or playlists you've created, it probably means that the settings on your computer were changed at some point. In order to switch settings back to Auto-Sync (and automatically open iTunes when an iPod is connected to your computer), you should check for the correct settings in the iTunes software.

Note *When using the Auto-Sync feature, songs and playlists cannot be deleted from your iPod without first deleting them from the library or Source list of your iTunes software. In fact, when you click on an iPod in the Source list, you should notice that songs on the iPod are grayed out and you're unable to select them from the list.*

Follow these steps if the Auto-Sync feature is not working properly in iTunes:

1. **Connect an iPod to your computer using the Dock accessory or directly with a FireWire or USB 2.0 cable.**

2. **If it doesn't launch automatically, open the iTunes software by clicking on its application icon.**

3. **Select your iPod device in the Source list on the left side of the iTunes application window.**

4. **Click the Options button in the lower-right corner of the iTunes window.** The iTunes Preferences window appears with the iPod pane on display.

3.2 An iPod device in the iTunes Source list.

3.3 The Options button for an iPod provides access to choices for managing music.

5. **Make certain that the Automatically update all songs and playlists option, located at the top of the Music tab in the iPod Options window, is activated.**

6. **Click on the General tab to the right of the Music tab in the same iPod Options window.**

3.4 The Automatically update all songs and playlists option is the Auto-Sync feature.

7. **Check the Open iTunes when this iPod is attached option if it isn't already checked.** The next time you connect your iPod to the computer, if iTunes isn't running already, it will launch.

Adding songs and playlists manually

Although there is nothing wrong with the automatic method of transferring music, there are drawbacks, particularly if you like to manage files on the iPod's hard drive, or you want to use an iPod on multiple computers. In fact, manually managing your music (the second method for transferring songs and playlists) is really the best way to gain access to an iPod's most interesting uses, beyond just music and photos. As far as copy protection of music is concerned, it's also the only way to utilize songs from your computer at home and your machine at work. If you own the music, why shouldn't you be able to play it on every computer and device you own? The Auto-Sync feature was created to placate the record labels with a method that prevents a user from easily plugging in his iPod on a friend's computer and copying her music. Fortunately, there is a way around the Auto-Sync feature (for legal purposes of course), which requires only a few simple steps to prepare.

3.5 The General tab in the iPod Options window contains the option for automatically launching iTunes when an iPod is connected to the computer — a useful option, particularly for the Auto-Sync feature.

Follow these steps to manually manage the transfer of songs and playlists:

1. **Connect an iPod to your computer using the Dock accessory or directly with a FireWire or USB 2.0 cable.**

2. **If it doesn't launch automatically, open the iTunes software by double-clicking on its application icon.**

3. **Select your iPod device in the Source list on the left side of the iTunes application window.**

4. **Click the Options button in the lower-right corner of the iTunes application window.**

5. **Select the Manually manage songs and playlists option, located toward the bottom of the Music tab in the iPod Options window.**

6. **Locate songs or playlists in iTunes and drag them onto the iPod icon in the Source list.** Songs and playlists have now been added manually to your iPod device and function the same as songs or playlists added with Auto-Sync.

3.6 Use the Manually manage songs and playlists option if you want to deactivate the Auto-Sync feature, which limits your file-sharing and file-copying abilities.

Deleting songs and playlists manually

Once an iPod has been set up to manually manage music, adding songs (as described in the preceding section) and deleting them is easy. To delete songs and playlists manually, follow these steps:

1. **Make certain your iPod is connected, the iTunes software is open, and the option to manage the iPod manually has been selected (as described in the preceding set of steps).**

2. **Select your iPod device in the Source list, located on the left side of the iTunes application window.**

3. **Choose a song or playlist to remove.**

4. **Press the Delete key on your computer's keyboard to remove the song or playlist.** Deleting songs removes them from the iPod, although songs included in a deleted playlist are not removed — only the playlist describing the songs to play is removed.

Creating On-The-Go Playlists

Songs in a playlist can be organized in any combination that you want and are not limited by categories like album, artist, or genre. Any number of arrangements you can think of are possible. Usually, playlists are created in iTunes, where it's easiest to type new names for playlists, as well as simply drag-and-drop songs into them.

Although iTunes is the ideal place to create your playlists, you can also create them on the iPod itself using On-The-Go playlists. If you forgot to set up a new playlist in iTunes for your commute to work, you can quickly design one on the go while traveling on the train or before you leave the office.

 Cross-Reference *For more information on iTunes, see Chapter 4.*

The following steps describe how to create an On-The-Go playlist:

1. **Using your iPod's Click Wheel controls, locate the first song you want to add to an On-The-Go playlist.**

2. **When you've found a song, highlight it, and then press and hold the center Select button on the Click Wheel until the song's name flashes.** You may select and add individual songs or entire albums to an On-The-Go playlist using this method.

3. **Continue locating and selecting songs for your playlist as described in Step 2.** Each song is added to the playlist in the order in which you select them.

4. **When you finish selecting songs, return to the Music menu and choose Playlists.** The Playlists menu screen appears.

5. **Scroll down to the bottom of the Playlists menu screen and choose On-The-Go.** The On-The-Go menu screen appears.

3.7 Choose On-The-Go to view the playlist you instantly created on the iPod without resorting to iTunes.

6. **Select the first song in the list and press the center Select button to begin playing your newly created playlist in its entirety, or select any song to play from that point forward.**

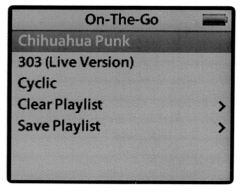

3.8 Choose a song from the On-The-Go playlist you have created.

Tip *You can remove an On-The-Go playlist by selecting Clear Playlist from the On-The-Go menu page.*

Shuffling Songs

One of the most used playback features on an iPod (and the inspiration for the diminutive iPod shuffle) is the shuffle feature. Shuffling randomly selects songs from your entire iPod library and plays them. Because the iPod (and iTunes software) keeps track of exactly when a song has been played, it can avoid playing the same songs close together. Using the shuffle feature makes listening to an iPod fun, because you never know what song it's going to play next. It's like having your own private DJ. You may even be pleasantly surprised by some of the combinations of songs it comes up with. To activate the shuffle feature simply select Shuffle Songs from the main iPod menu. If you're using an iPod shuffle, the default option is to shuffle songs or, if you've put your shuffle into sequential mode, you can flip the switch back into shuffle mode (bottom position) to reactivate the feature.

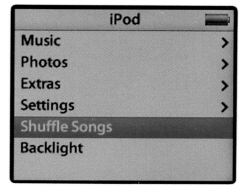

3.9 The iPod's Shuffle Songs feature is one of the most used playback options.

Rating Songs

Ratings are a way to help you remember what songs you like most and to assist in the sorting of Smart Playlists (discussed in Chapter 4), which can be used to create a playlist of songs that match your criteria for what is considered good, bad, or favorite music. There is also a default Top-Rated Songs playlist on your iPod that lists your music in order of its rating. You can add ratings to a song as it plays on your iPod.

Follow these steps to apply a rating to songs on your iPod:

1. **Begin playing a song that you want to rate.** The Now Playing screen appears with the song information displayed.

2. **While the song is playing, press the center Select button twice.** The timeline is replaced by a set of dots (or stars, if you've already rated the song).

3. **Use the Click Wheel to scroll right to add stars to or left to delete stars from the rating of a song.**

3.10 Ratings for a song range from no stars to five stars.

4. **Press the center Select button to accept the new rating and return to the Now Playing screen.**

Using iPod's Calendar and Contacts

All iPod models (with the exception of iPod shuffle, which does not have a screen) come with special utilities that add some productivity features to the iPod. Although it isn't the primary function of an iPod (after all, it's built for fun, not work), you can use the Calendar and Contacts features to keep track of important dates, work schedules, or address book information. An iPod keeps not only your songs organized, but your life as well. Unfortunately, you cannot enter information into the iPod, because it lacks an input device, like a basic keyboard. However, you can download calendar and contacts information from other applications on your computer into the iPod for viewing while away from home. In addition, a calendar, even without specific appointments entered into it, can be useful for finding dates (April 17, 2006, is a Monday, for example).

Note *If you're using a Mac, iTunes 4.8 or later provides an interface to synchronize your Address Book contacts and iCal calendars automatically. However, you can drag vCard contact information or vCalendar or iCalendar format calendar data from any application on Mac or Windows that supports those standards.*

The following steps demonstrate where to access the calendar.

1. **From the iPod's main menu, choose Extras ⇨ Calendar ⇨ All.** The screen displays a calendar.

2. **Scroll through the dates with the Click Wheel controls.** Scrolling beyond the beginning and end dates for a particular month automatically opens the next or previous months calendar.

II	Apr 2005					▬
Sun	Mon	Tue	Wed	Thu	Fri	Sat
27	28	29	30	31	1	2
3	4	5	6	7	8	9
10	11	12	13	14	15	16
17	18	19	20	21	22	23
24	25	26	27	28	29	30
1	2	3	4	5	6	7

3.11 The iPod's Calendar feature.

3. **To view information for a specific date, press the Select button to see details for that day.** Dates with notes or appointments added to them appear with a dot inside them on the calendar.

The following steps demonstrate where to access the contacts.

1. **From the iPod main menu screen, choose Extras.** The Extras menu screen appears.

2. **Scroll up the Extras menu screen to the Contacts option and press the Select button.** Any contacts that you've added to your iPod appear in a list, similar to the appearance of songs or albums.

3. **Press the Select button to view information for a specific contact.** The contact details for the selected entry appear.

4. **When you finish viewing contact information, press the Menu button a few times to return to the main menu.**

3.12 The iPod's Contact feature.

Using iPod as an Alarm Clock or Sleep Timer

Among its many practical uses, an iPod may be used as an alarm clock or to help you fall asleep, with the use of the built-in Alarm Clock or Sleep Timer features. This is great for travelers, the occasional nap at work, or for anyone that wants to fall asleep or awaken to the sounds of his favorite music.

Setting the iPod's Alarm Clock

The Alarm feature allows you to set a specific time for a beep or music to turn on. This feature works like an ordinary clock, with the advantage of using music instead of a startling, electronic noise.

The following steps demonstrate how to set the alarm on an iPod.

1. **From the iPod's main menu, choose Extras ➪ Clock ➪ Alarm Clock.** The Alarm Clock menu screen appears.

2. **Scroll down and choose Time.** A time display appears on the screen.

3. **Move your thumb clockwise or counterclockwise around the Click Wheel to select an appropriate time for the alarm.**

4. **Click the center Select button on the Click Wheel when you've arrived at the desired time.** Your alarm time is now set and you're returned to the Alarm Clock menu.

5. **Scroll up and choose Alarm.** Clicking on the Alarm option toggles between On or Off.

6. **Scroll down and choose Sound.** You're presented with a list of all the playlists on your iPod, as well as the standard Beep. The Beep uses the simple, built-in sound on the iPod (like the Clicker, only a different tone). Playlists require headphones or a separate speaker device, because they don't use the built-in speaker.

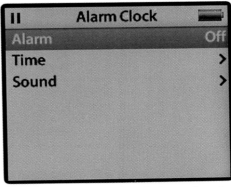

3.13 iPod's alarm clock includes options for Alarm (On or Off), Time, and Sound.

 For details about external speakers, check out some of the Bose or JBL speaker systems discussed in Chapter 6.

7. **After you've selected the Beep or a playlist, press the center Select button on the Click Wheel to accept the choice and return to the previous menu.** Your alarm will now go off at the appointed time, playing your selection or beeping.

Setting the iPod's Sleep Timer

If you're the type of person who likes to fall asleep to music, or even white noise, the iPod's Sleep Timer should be exactly what you need. Simply set the timer for a specified period of time (15 minutes for example), activate the timer, and start your music or prerecorded soothing sounds (waves, waterfalls, and so on). With the Sleep Timer, you no longer have to worry about wasting the iPod's battery by leaving it on all night.

The following steps demonstrate how to utilize the iPod's Sleep Timer.

1. **From the iPod's main menu, choose Extras ➪ Clock ➪ Sleep Timer.**

2. **Scroll down and choose a duration of time.** This is the amount of time that will pass before the iPod turns off. Choices include Off (the default option, which deactivates the feature), 15, 30, 60, 90, and 120 Minutes.

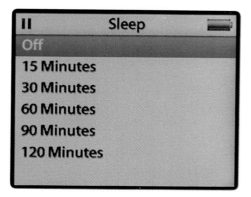

3.14 Choose an appropriate duration for the Sleep Timer.

3. **Click the center Select button on the Click Wheel when you've arrived at the desired duration.** This activates the timer and returns you to the previous menu.

4. **Choose a song, album, or playlist.** You can now fall asleep, secure in the knowledge that your iPod's battery won't be drained by the time you wake up.

Using iPod as a Hard Drive

In addition to holding songs, playlists, and photos, an iPod can be used as a hard drive to hold data, or files copied from a computer. You can use an iPod as you would any other portable, FireWire, or USB hard drive. Files can be easily dragged and dropped onto the volume and transported from one computer to another. This feature is useful for transferring files between work and home, or for keeping a backup of important documents. With an iPod, you can carry all your Microsoft Word, Excel, and PowerPoint documents; Adobe Acrobat PDFs; QuickTime movies; or any other type of file, in addition to your music and digital photos. Students and professional users can always keep a copy of important documents with them wherever they go. In fact, scientists have used iPods to carry a copy of the entire human genome, and filmmakers like Peter Jackson have used iPods to send copies of special effects sequences around the world. The only limit to what you can carry is the capacity of your iPod's hard drive. If you intend to use your iPod as a hard drive, make certain you leave a few extra gigabytes of space for use later on.

Take the following steps to copy files from your computer onto an iPod. Some of the initial steps are for first-time users. When your iPod and iTunes software are set up to manage files manually, the process for simply copying files should be faster.

1. **Connect an iPod to your computer using the Dock accessory or directly with a FireWire or USB 2.0 cable.**

2. **If it doesn't launch automatically, open the iTunes software by clicking on its application icon.**

3. **Select your iPod device in the Source list on the left side of the application window.**

4. **Click the Options button in the lower-right corner of the iTunes window.** The iPod Options window appears.

5. **Select the Manually manage songs and playlists option, located toward the bottom of the Music tab in the iPod Options window.** Manually managing your music automatically enables the use of your iPod as a hard drive.

6. **Click on the General tab toward the top of the same iPod Options window.**

7. **Select the Enable disk use option if it isn't already selected.** You already enabled disk

use when you chose to manually manage songs and playlists. However, with the Enable disk use option checked, you may also use the Auto-Sync feature and automatically update your iTunes songs and playlists, while still using your iPod as a hard drive. If you decide to use the Auto-Sync feature, don't select the Manually manage songs and playlists option.

8. **Deselect the Open iTunes when this iPod is attached option if it is selected.** If you intend to use your iPod regularly as a hard drive, it may be easier to not launch iTunes automatically each time an iPod is connected to your computer.

9. **Double-click the iPod icon that appears on your desktop as a hard drive volume (on a Mac) or in the list of available drives on a PC.**

10. **Locate files or folders on your hard drive and drag them onto the open iPod volume.**

Caution   *Do not drag music files and photos you want to play or view onto an iPod volume. These files are only playable if they're added through the iTunes software, and they should not utilize the hard drive feature as described here.*

3.15 Using the iPod as a hard drive.

You can use an iPod shuffle as a hard drive, just as you would any other iPod. In the same way, you need to make certain the Enable disk use option is activated in the Options menu for the device (located in iTunes as described in the previous section). When an iPod shuffle is in hard disk mode, its status light blinks orange and its disk icon appears on the desktop (Mac) or in the Windows Explorer window (PC). This indicates that files can be dragged and dropped onto the volume as you would for any other iPod or hard drive.

Reading Notes on an iPod

Because an iPod can be used as a hard drive, any type of files may be stored on it, in addition to ordinary music and photo files. In addition, there is a special extra folder on an iPod that allows short text files to be stored and read through the iPod's built-in screen. Notes are a convenient way to carry around shopping lists, directions, outlines, presentations, study sheets, e-mails, essays, books (broken into parts), or other reminders.

 Note *Individual notes are limited to a size of 4K. While this size is rather small, you may include as many different notes as you can fit into the Notes folder on your iPod's hard drive. Larger notes can be broken into smaller files and read in parts.*

1. **Create a text document in your word processing application of choice, including TextEdit (Mac), Notes (PC), Microsoft Word, and others.**

2. **Save your document as a text file.** These are usually delineated by a .txt extension.

3. **Connect your iPod to the computer using the Dock accessory or directly with a FireWire or USB 2.0 cable.** If the Enable disk use or Manually manage songs and playlists options have been activated (as described in the previous sections), your iPod should be ready to use as a hard drive. The iPod volume should appear as an icon on your desktop or in the list of available drives on your PC.

4. **Double-click the iPod icon to open the hard drive.**

5. **Locate any text files you want to use and drag them into the Notes folder on your iPod.**

6. **From the iPod's main menu, choose Extras – Notes, and select the particular note you want to read.**

 Cross-Reference *Refer to Chapter 7 for information on adding links between note files on your iPod.*

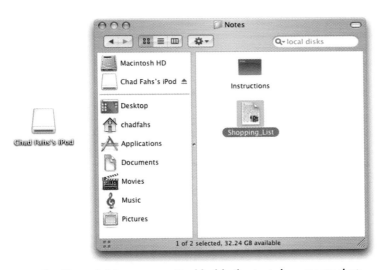

3.16 The Notes folder on your iPod holds the text documents that you can read on its screen.

Playing Games on an iPod

Each iPod, with the exception of the iPod shuffle of course, includes a few games for passing the time while waiting for a plane or relaxing on the couch. Currently, the default games that come with an iPod are very simple and lack complexity (think early Atari), although no claims have ever been made about the iPod's use as a gaming machine. But, for your next trip to a doctor's waiting room, use your iPod to pass the time. Included on the iPod are classics like Solitaire, Parachute, Brick (similar to Breakout or Arachnoid), and Music Quiz. The Music Quiz game, which randomly chooses a list of songs from your collection, plays a ten-second snippet of one song and asks you to identify it, is actually interesting and addictive.

Follow these directions to locate and play a game on your iPod.

1. **From the iPod's main menu, choose Extras ➪ Games.** The Games menu screen appears.

2. **Press the Select button to play a game, such as Music Quiz.** The game will begin.

3. **If the game doesn't begin immediately, press the Select button.** The Music Quiz game is an exception to this rule, because it starts up as soon as you select it.

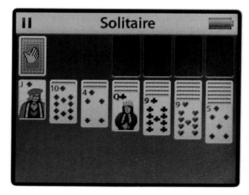

3.17 The iPod includes some basic games to help pass time.

Working with iPod Software

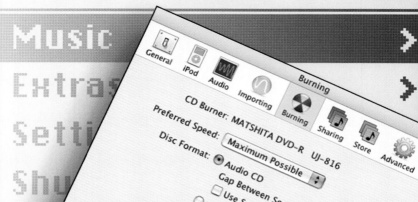

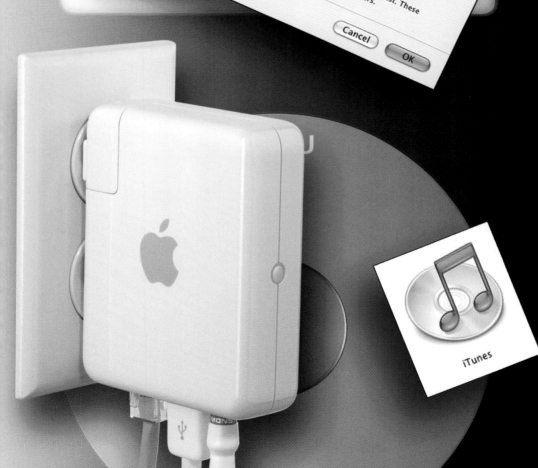

iTunes Basics and More

The iPod is an amazing device. But without iTunes software or some other program designed to interface with your iPod, it's much less useful, particularly for listening to music. From its release, the iPod has had a close familial relationship with iTunes. Apple is constantly adding new features to iTunes to make your iPod even more useful and new features to the iPod that take advantage of iTunes features—it's a delicious (not vicious) circle. In this chapter, I discuss leveraging iTunes to help you better organize, manage, and play the music files you place on your iPod.

About iTunes

iTunes, shown in figure 4.1, is the hub of your digital music environment. Although the iPod is your portable music player, iTunes is your music manager. In addition to helping you import, organize, transfer, share, and download music, iTunes is also a music jukebox, allowing you to listen to music on your computer or streamed wirelessly to other locations in your home through the use of Airport Express hardware. iTunes software is the bridge to the iTunes Music Store, the revolutionary service that lets you purchase music online. Because iTunes is one of the few software applications produced by Apple that runs on other platforms, Windows users can now experience the power and simplicity that is synonymous with Apple.

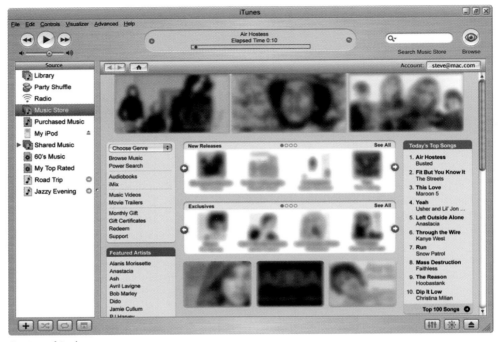

Courtesy of Apple

4.1 Apple's iTunes software is a powerful music hub for your desktop or laptop computer, which even allows access to a world of online music through the iTunes Music Store, pictured here for the United Kingdom.

Supported Audio Formats

Your choice of audio format determines a lot about how you can use your music. You might choose one format because it allows you to fit several thousand songs on your iPod, and another format that preserves the quality of the original source material better but takes up more space. iTunes supports a wide variety of audio formats and easily converts one format to another. Before you take a look at the most commonly supported audio formats, it's important to consider a few important properties that are related to each codec (compressor-decompressor) and the results you can expect.

About compression

When you convert an audio file from one format to another, compression is often applied. *Compression* makes your audio files more manageable, but it can also degrade the quality of your audio. Formats that cause data to be lost are referred to as *lossy*, and after the data is removed from the file, it cannot be retrieved. Fortunately, the majority of commonly used lossy formats, such as those discussed in this chapter, are actually quite good, and most listeners cannot hear the difference.

Compression is a fact of life in the world of computers. Information is sacrificed all the time, whether when working with video, graphics, or even audio. As computers become faster and storage cheaper and more plentiful, the need for added compression is reduced. However, most modern compression schemes are very good at removing only those portions of information that are imperceptible to human vision or hearing. In fact, many times you'll never be aware that anything is missing, particularly when it comes to music. The ear is very forgiving, and audio quality so high in general, that many compressed formats (even the lossy kind) are virtually identical. The real dilemma occurs when you want to recompress a file to another lossy format. This compounds the loss of quality, which is exponentially removed from the original source file — such as the audio taken from a CD or photos taken from a digital camera. Whichever format you choose, make certain that you'll be satisfied with your decision without needing to recompress the file later on. If you have the option, make certain that you keep the *master* (the file you originally extracted your audio from), in case you decide to recompress your files using a better format. After all, technology is changing every day, and the format you choose this week might be usurped next week by a better, higher-quality alternative. Unfortunately, there is no easy way to convert the audio you purchase from the iTunes Music Store or other online sites to a better format, because most services don't allow you to download music a second time without paying for a new copy.

 Note *You can convert your iTunes audio to an uncompressed format, such as AIFF, by burning it to an audio CD. However, you do not gain any quality by doing so, because the original compression applied to the file cannot be reversed.*

Bit rates

All audio files play by transferring data and the speed at which they transfer data is called the bit rate, whether they're used with iTunes or created and exported from a different application. The bit rate is one of the factors that determines the amount of data, or storage space, that a file occupies. When the file is accessed by iTunes, QuickTime, or something similar (whether software- or hardware-based), the bit rate determines how much data is required to make that file play. If the bit rate is high, more data must pass through the system at one time, which can cause problems for slower machines and results in larger file sizes that are more difficult to store and work with.

When choosing an audio file format, make sure that its bit rate meets the requirements of your particular setup, particularly in terms of storage space. Because most users have very large hard drives (prices per gigabyte are getting lower every day), space is not as much of an issue, unless you're placing your entire music collection on your iPod mini or iPod shuffle. Also, remember that bit rates may vary according to format and compression settings. Some formats are more efficient and can produce higher-quality files at lower bit rates. For example, an AAC file's 128 Kbps bit rate is the standard for the iTunes Music Store and sounds good. However, an equivalent MP3 file would require about one-and-a-half times that bit rate to achieve a similar level of quality.

Sample rate

The sample rate for an audio file can have a tremendous effect on its quality. Samples indicate the number of units that an analog audio waveform is broken into (this applies to sound waves that are captured and manipulated by digital devices). The greater the number of samples, the smaller these units become. Smaller samples result in greater quality, because more detail is recorded. You can think of this like a ruler. Centimeter markings on a ruler may be sufficient, yet millimeter markings would record more detail about the object you're measuring. Thus, the finer your units of measure (or samples) the greater the fidelity of your measurements.

An audio file with a sample rate of 22 kHz is about half as good as a 44.1 kHz file, which is what we associate with CD-quality sound. Digital camcorders and DVDs use an even higher sample rate of about 48 kHz for their audio. The higher the sample rate, the more accurate the sampled audio. For most music files, the 44.1 kHz sample rate of compact discs is sufficient. In fact, it is virtually impossible to tell the difference between 44.1 and higher sample rates — unless you're an audiophile with high-quality speakers. In addition, the higher your sample rate, the more space that is required to store your files (this is similar to the situation with bit rates, which also add to the amount of storage as they get higher).

iPod users should generally keep their music at 44.1 kHz, although there are times when some users may want to store their music at 48 kHz to retain audio from a DVD or for video-editing purposes (see figure 4.2) or at 22 kHz for long, spoken-word passages, which do not require as much dynamic range as music. The iTunes Preferences Importing pane is where you choose an encoder and the bit-rate, sample rate, number of channels, and stereo mode. If you choose an encoder, and then choose Custom from the Setting pop-up menu, you will see a dialog box similar to the one in figure 4.2.

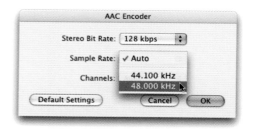

4.2 The custom settings for an encoder in iTunes Preferences window allow you to specify bit rate and sample rate for the audio files you're importing.

The size or bit width of your samples also has an effect on quality. A 16-bit sample, for instance, is used by standard CDs and is generally the standard for high-quality digital audio. All of your music should be 16-bit, although there are higher formats that are not suited for iPod or iTunes but are used by audio professionals for recording and mastering purposes (2-bit audio, for example). At high levels, the difference in quality is essentially indistinguishable. However, when working with sample settings that are below 16-bit, there can be a marked difference in quality.

Unless you're using audio that is strictly spoken word and the quality is not an issue, you should avoid using 8-bit audio (for example, you recorded from a low-quality source and just want to fit as much spoken word as possible on a disc or hard drive), although 12-bit might be acceptable on occasion. 8-bit audio might be acceptable for recorded voice memos or audio lectures, to conserve as much space as possible. Due to its small file size, 8-bit audio would be suitable for transferring over the Internet or transmitting by mobile device. In general, always keep your music and other sound files at 16-bit if you don't want a lot of noise in your audio.

AAC

The default audio codec for iTunes on both Macs and PCs is AAC, or Advanced Audio Coding, and is a part of the MPEG-4 specifications (see figure 4.3). This format was created by a group of companies that includes Dolby, AT&T, Sony, and Nokia (among others); this group was also responsible for the creation of MP3 and AC3 Dolby Digital (frequently used for DVDs).

 Note *Apple's Fair Play DRM is employed with iTMS files, giving them a file extension of* .m4p *(mpeg-4, protected), whereas the AAC files you create do not employ DRM and have an extension of* .m4a *(mpeg-4 audio).*

It is this engineering prowess that allowed AAC to exceed the quality of earlier codecs, such as MP3, at lower bit rates. Because AAC can reproduce sound that, at least to most ears, is indistinguishable from the original audio source, while keeping file sizes manageable, it has been chosen to be the official format of the iTunes Music Store. At 128 Kbps, the efficiency of AAC makes it easily downloadable, even over a slow Internet connection. As Apple puts it, "Small files. Large sounds."

01 Let Go.m4a

4.3 Apple's AAC format is the lossy format utilized by the iTunes Music Store and an improvement over previous compressed formats, such as MP3.

AIFF

Uncompressed audio files, like those on a CD, employ what is called PCM (pulse-coded modulation). Depending on which computer platform you're using or the type of software the files were created with, the digital presentation on your computer might vary. For Macs, uncompressed audio files most often come as an AIFF file and on a Windows computer, they will usually be WAV files.

When ripping audio from a CD, without applying compression that converts it to AAC, MP3, or another codec, your music arrives as a file with the extension .aiff or .aif. Because they're uncompressed, these files are inefficient in terms of the storage space they require. For this reason, AIFF files are almost always converted to AAC (or equivalent) for playback on an iPod. However, if you want to retain full quality on an audio file, it should remain as an AIFF (or employ the Apple Lossless codec), at least as a backup. For example, if you've created audio using GarageBand (Apple's audio application in the iLife suite of software), or if you've exported audio from a video project you were working on in Final Cut Pro or iMovie, it should be in the AIFF format. You can think of AIFF (see figure 4.4) as a master format for the Mac, from which all other audio formats can be derived.

01 Let Go.aif

4.4 AIFF is the uncompressed audio format for Macs.

MP3

MP3 is the format most often associated with portable music players and songs downloaded from the Internet (see figure 4.5). When MP3s were first introduced, they were a revolution, particularly because they maintained excellent sound quality in an easily downloadable form (although transferring over a dial-up Internet connection was always less than ideal). They spawned a file-swapping craze in the '90s, led by services like Napster.

Although not as efficient as AAC (Apple's alternate format), MP3 codecs still do a decent job of producing manageable file sizes while maintaining much of your audio's original quality. Of course, in order to get good results, you must increase the bit rate, usually to levels much higher than AAC. For example, a 192 Kbps MP3 file is often necessary to approximate the quality of a 128 Kbps AAC file.

WAV

WAV, WAVE, or a .wav file is the uncompressed audio format created by Microsoft and Intel, and used primarily on PCs (although Macs read them just fine). The quality of a WAV file is the same as an AIFF, and depending what type of computer you're working on, it's the format that is produced by music ripped directly from a CD without compression applied.

You can use WAV files for a variety of purposes, although they're ideally suited to multimedia applications, where you require high-quality audio that may later be recompressed to fit a particular playback device (such as sound effects for games, movies, Flash animations, or audio archives). Storing files in WAV format takes a lot of space, so it's generally impractical for large quantities of audio. However, if you have the space and your project requires the cleanest audio you can afford, WAV is a good option (see figure 4.6).

12 Let Go.mp3

4.5 MP3 is still a popular lossy format for Web audio and personal digital music players (such as the iPod), although MP3 is generally not as efficient or as high quality as AAC.

01 Let Go.wav

4.6 WAV is the uncompressed audio format for PCs.

You can load uncompressed WAV files onto an iPod, although your device fills up fast if you have a lot of files. Still, it's nice to know that you can include WAV and AIFF files on an iPod and in iTunes, in case you need them for a video project, or you simply have a favorite CD that you want to store in the best possible format. If you happen to borrow a CD from a family member or friend, you might consider ripping it in WAV format first (or AIFF) and then recompressing into AAC or MP3 for use on your iPod. This way, you at least have the full-quality master for burning a perfect CD or recompressing later if a file is lost on your iPod or simply goes bad and needs re-encoding.

Apple Lossless

Although the majority of digital formats require some type of lossy compression to make files small enough to be manageable for use on a computer and other electronic devices, some formats apply compression without sacrificing the quality or integrity of the original audio. One of the newest lossless compression (lossless meaning it doesn't lose data like a lossy file does) formats is called Apple Lossless.

By using Apple Lossless compression, you can reduce the file size of an uncompressed audio file to about half of the original file size (AIFF or WAV files ripped from a CD). This allows you to keep the original quality of your audio while reducing the amount of space required to store them. For example, you could import and store your entire CD collection on a series of large hard drives in the Apple Lossless format, and then make all subsequent format conversions to AAC or MP3 using these master files. This method of working is impractical for the majority of users, although it is a nice option to have if you're concerned about keeping digital archives or pristine audio, without sacrificing

the amount of space required by a CD. Of course, you can also play back these files directly from an iPod, taking pristine-quality music wherever you go; that said, there are a few drawbacks, such as less space for other music, photos, and other files, as well as limited skip protection.

A single audio CD holds a maximum of 74 or 80 minutes of audio (740MB to 800MB). Using Apple Lossless brings down the storage requirements to 370 to 400MB. In this scenario, you can fit almost three CDs' worth of audio in a single gigabyte. For example, a 300GB hard drive might fit a minimum of 900 or more audio CDs without sacrificing any quality. Choose iTunes ⇨ Preferences and click the Importing icon. The dialog box shown in figure 4.7 appears and you can choose Apple Lossless from the Import Using pop-up menu.

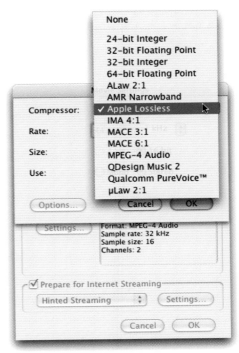

4.7 Apple Lossless is a new format from Apple that cuts the file sizes of audio in half without losing any quality.

Setting iTunes Preferences

In order to use iTunes properly, you must configure it to suit your needs. In most cases, you use the preferences to make the necessary adjustments. This might include changing the way that iTunes reacts to a CD placed in your computer, the codec that is used to import it, or features of the iTunes Music Store you want to access. There are a variety of settings that can be made in the iTunes Preferences windows, many of which are discussed in this section. Begin by opening the preferences window (iTunes ➪ Preferences), and then referring to the headings that follow for more information on a particular category.

General

The General pane, shown in figure 4.8, is the first preferences pane that you see when opening the iTunes Preferences. This is where you set most of the standard settings for iTunes:

✦ **Source Text.** This option allows you to choose the size of the source text. Options are Small and Large.

✦ **Song Text.** Change this option to select the size for your song text. Options are Small or Large.

✦ **Show.** Check various items in this category to show up in your iTunes Source list when iTunes is opened. You can select to show Party Shuffle, Radio, Show genre when browsing, Group compilations when browsing, and Show links to Music Store.

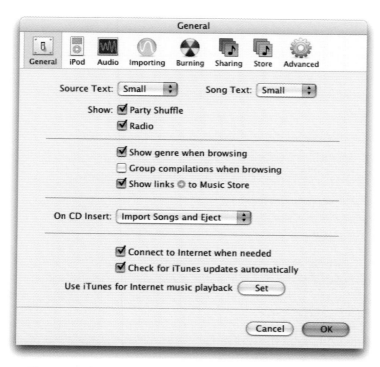

4.8 The General pane of the iTunes Preferences window.

✦ **On CD Insert.** Your choice for this option determines what happens when you insert an audio CD into your computer while iTunes is running. Choices include Import Songs and Eject, Show Songs, Begin Playing, and Import Songs.

✦ **Connect to the Internet when needed.** Select this option to allow iTunes to connect your computer to the Internet when it needs to retrieve updates or song information or access the iTunes Music Store.

✦ **Check for iTunes updates automatically.** If you want iTunes to check for software updates, select this option.

✦ **Use iTunes for Internet music playback.** Select this option if you want to play music from the Internet through iTunes instead of another application (such as QuickTime).

iPod

Options in the iPod pane of the Preferences window only appear when an iPod is connected to your computer. With an iPod connected, you should see the name of your iPod with two tabs beneath: Music and General.

The Music tab in the iPod Options pane includes preferences for how your music is synced (as shown in figure 4.9):

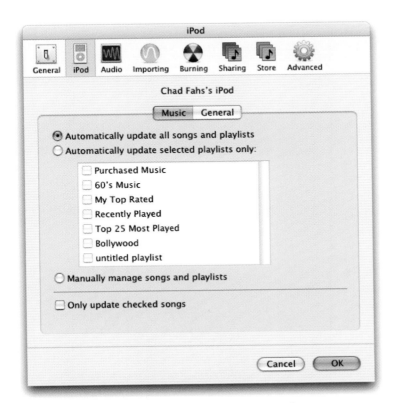

4.9 The iPod section of the iTunes Preferences window.

✦ **Automatically update all songs and playlists.** By default, all songs and playlists are automatically updated (this is the Auto-Sync feature touted by Apple). Deselect this option if you do not want to automatically update.

✦ **Automatically update selected playlists only.** You can choose to update just selected playlists by selecting this option. Your current playlists are listed below this option and will become active choices when this option is selected.

✦ **Manually manage songs and playlists.** Select this option if you would prefer to manage your songs and playlists.

Tip

There is an advantage to updating manually—you can easily work with multiple computers without having your iPod associate itself with just one machine. If you were to use the Automatically update all songs and playlists option, when you connect your iPod to a computer that is not your own, it will attempt to replace the music it currently contains with the music on the other computer. Employing manual updating allows you to add selected songs from the second computer without wiping out your music library.

✦ **Only update checked songs.** Selecting this option tells iTunes not to transfer songs whose checkboxes in the song list are unchecked.

When you click the General tab, you're presented with two options.

✦ **Open iTunes when this iPod is attached.** This is the default choice; it simply gets you into

iTunes faster when hooking up or syncing your iPod.

✦ **Enable disk use.** This option is usually activated when you manually manage your music, although you can use it even with the automatic-update feature running. Disk use simply means that your iPod appears as a mounted device on your computer, allowing you to copy files onto it as you would any other hard drive. This is convenient for transferring files back and forth from work to your home, or for storing importing data, such as homework, presentations, or anything else you might need.

Note

If you connect your iPod while the Preferences window is still open, the device may not be recognized right away in the iPod section. (A message that says iPod not connected appears when an iPod is not detected.) Close the Preferences window and open it again to see options for your iPod, if this happens.

Depending on what version of iTunes you're running and what model iPod you have, you might also encounter Photos, Podcasts, Contacts, and Calendars tabs in the iPod pane. All four of these tabs are analogous to the iPod pane's Music tab as follows:

✦ **Photos.** This tab appears if you have an iPod photo attached and lets you specify whether your iPhoto Library or selected albums (Mac) or Photoshop Elements 3/ Adobe Photoshop Album (Windows) collections are to be downloaded. You can also specify individual folders of images on either platform for synchronization.

✦ **Podcasts.** This is a new tab introduced with iTunes 4.9 that lets you specify which, if any, of your podcasts should be downloaded to the iPod and when (or whether) specified podcasts should be removed.

✦ **Contacts.** This tab only appears when connected to a Mac (iTunes 4.8 or newer) and controls synchronization of Address Book data.

✦ **Calendars.** This is also Mac and iTunes 4.8 or later specific and provides the interface between the iCal application's data and your iPod.

As Apple frequently adds new models and capabilities, this list could well grow by the time you read the book.

Audio

The Audio pane of the Preferences window, shown in figure 4.10, includes a few options for the way sound is played through iTunes.

✦ **Crossfade playback.** This option creates smooth transitions from one song to the next. This option is turned on by default and its setting in the middle is a good balance.

✦ **Sound Enhancer.** This feature can add depth to your audio. You can adjust the amount of the effect by raising or lowering its slider.

✦ **Sound Check.** This option makes the volume of your songs play at the same levels for consistency, although songs are usually

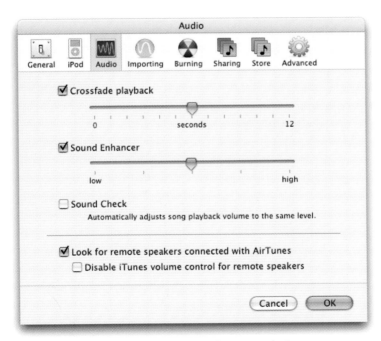

4.10 The Audio pane of the iTunes Preferences window.

mastered at levels that were meant to accentuate the dynamics, not even them out. This option is unchecked by default.

✦ **Look for remote speakers connected with AirTunes.** Selecting this option tells iTunes to look for speakers hooked up in other locations of your house through AirPort Express.

✦ **Disable iTunes volume control for remote speakers.** Selecting this option does just what it says — it disables the iTunes ability to control the volume of remote speakers connected through AirPort Express.

Importing

The Importing pane of the Preferences window, shown in figure 4.11, is where you make choices about the type of encoder that is used to import your music. Your options include:

✦ **Import Using.** Choose an import file type that iTunes will use as the default. Your choices include AAC Encoder, MP3, Apple Lossless, WAV, and AIFF.

✦ **Setting.** Choose from a quality setting appropriate to the encoder chosen. For example, MP3 offers, Good (128 Kbps), High (160 Kbps), Higher (192 Kbps), and Custom. The specifics about the choice you make for Setting appear in the Details box below that option.

✦ **Play songs while importing.** Select this option if you would like to hear the songs you are importing while they are being imported.

✦ **Create file names with track number.** This option is selected by default and prepends the track number to the name when you rip a CD.

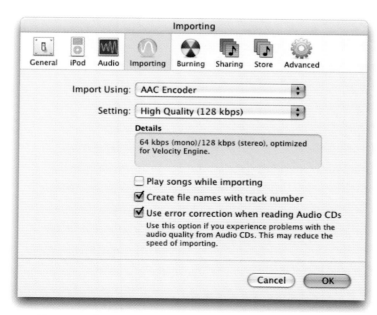

4.11 The Importing pane of the iTunes Preferences window.

✦ **Use error correction when reading Audio CDs.** This option is selected by default. Error correction is generally best left on, because you want to make certain that any skips or hiccups in the importing process do not cause bad data in your audio files. (Nobody wants to re-import damaged music.)

Burning

The Burning pane of the Preferences window presents choices for how you create CDs or DVDs with your music files on them. Choices for burning, as shown in figure 4.12, include:

✦ **CD Burner.** The name of your CD burner should appear here. If you do not see a name here, it means that iTunes cannot find a burner with which it knows how to communicate.

✦ **Preferred Speed.** Depending on your system setup and the type of drive that is connected, you may be able to choose a preferred speed for the write time. Maximum Possible is usually best, unless your system is prone to errors and experiences write problems. Other choices include 1x, 2x, 4x, and so forth, depending on the speeds of which your burner is capable.

✦ **Disc Format.** Choose the type of media you are writing to. Select from Audio CD, MP3 CD, or Data CD or DVD. If you select Audio CD, you can determine the amount of time between songs and whether to use Sound Check. If you choose MP3 CD, you create a data (also known as an ISO 9660) CD of MP3 files that is playable in some, but far from all, standalone CD and DVD players. Choosing Data CD or DVD burns a backup data CD of the selected playlist.

4.12 The Burning pane of the iTunes Preferences window.

Sharing

The Sharing pane of the Preferences window has the preferences for sharing music across a network (see figure 4.13). Options in this pane include:

✦ **Look for shared music.** This option tells iTunes to check for other copies of iTunes on your LAN (local area network) that are sharing their music.

✦ **Share my music.** Select this option if you want to allow others in your network to access some or your entire music library. They can only listen to the music — they're not able to copy songs to their own machines.

- **Share entire library.** If you select this option, others in your network can access your entire library.

- **Share selected playlists.** When this option is selected, the playlists become active and you can choose a subset you want to share.

✦ **Shared name.** This option lets you specify a name by which your shared music will be known in the Source lists of those iTunes users with whom you're sharing.

✦ **Require password.** In order to protect access to your music, you can require that a password be entered before others can browse your collection.

4.13 The Sharing pane of the iTunes Preferences window.

Store

The Store pane of the Preferences window has the options for customizing your iTunes Music Store experience. These options only become available if the Show iTunes Music Store option is selected. The options shown in figure 4.14 include:

✦ **Buy and download using 1-Click.** When you select this option, it becomes your preferred method of purchasing songs through the iTunes Music Store. If you tend to buy single songs while visiting the store, 1-Click is convenient.

✦ **Buy using a Shopping Cart.** When you select this option, it becomes your preferred method of

purchasing songs through the iTunes Music Store. If you spend a long time per visit selecting multiple items, a shopping cart may be the best choice.

✦ **Play songs after downloading.** Select this option to begin playback immediately after downloading completes.

✦ **Load complete preview before playing.** If you're on a dial-up Internet connection, you may want to check this option. Doing so improves the playback performance of songs over a slow network connection.

4.14 The Store pane of the iTunes Preferences window.

Advanced

The Advanced pane of the Preferences window, shown in figure 4.15, is an area that you most likely will never need to go. But, if you are curious about what can be found on this pane, here are the options:

✦ **iTunes Music folder location.** This displays the location of your music. You should not change this option unless you are sure of what you're doing. For example, specifying a location to which you don't have read (or write) access will cause iTunes no end of problems when it is trying to manage your music. Similarly, placing the location on another volume will confuse iTunes if that volume is not present when iTunes launches or is dismounted while iTunes is running.

✦ **Streaming Buffer Size.** Choose a buffer size for streaming music from Music Store previews and Internet radio. Choices are Small, Medium, and Large.

✦ **Shuffle by.** Select either Song or Album as the standard shuffle option.

✦ **Keep iTunes Music folder organized.** This option is selected by default. It keeps your songs stored in a consistent manner.

✦ **Copy files to iTunes Music folder when adding to library.** This option is selected by default and does just what the name implies, making a copy of any song(s) added to the iTunes library inside the iTunes Music folder.

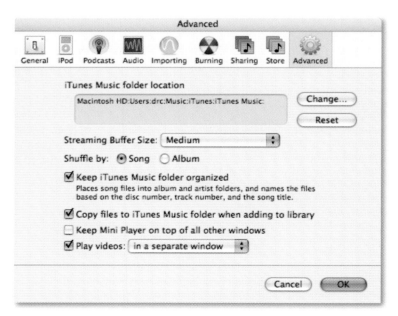

4.15 The Advanced pane of the iTunes Preferences window.

✦ **Keep Mini Player on top of all other windows.** When you reduce iTunes to the Mini Player window, it can easily be hidden by windows from other applications. Select this option if you want the Mini Player window to "float" above all other windows.

✦ **Play videos.** This option lets you specify whether music and other videos in your iTunes library, such as those downloaded from the iTunes Music Store, play in the main iTunes window, in a separate window, or full-screen. This feature only applies to iTunes 4.8 or later.

Setting view options

You can customize the column headings that are displayed in the iTunes window by choosing Edit ➪ View Options, as shown in figure 4.16 with the iTunes Library selected in the Source list. Although a certain number of categories are listed by default, you can easily change what is seen to suit your needs. For example, you might turn on a Year column to sort your songs by the years in which they were released. Click an option to select or deselect it. When you are done, click OK.

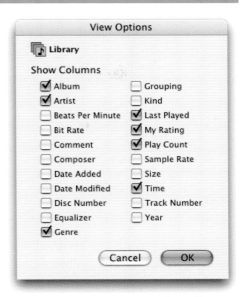

4.16 The View Options dialog box allows you to choose the columns of information that appear in the iTunes window.

Showing artwork

Any artwork or album covers that are associated with a particular song can be viewed from within the iTunes window. Simply choose Edit ➪ Show Artwork to open a special window in the bottom-left of the iTunes window, below the Source list (see figure 4.17). To hide the artwork, choose Edit ➪ Hide Artwork, or use the keyboard shortcut to toggle it on or off (⌘/Ctrl+G).

4.17 You can choose to display album covers for selected or currently playing songs.

Organizing Songs into Playlists

One of the best, most-often-used features of iTunes is the ability to build custom playlists of songs. *Playlists* are lists of songs that are put together in a specific order; it is kind of like putting together your own CD or album. With iTunes, you can create the virtual albums you always wanted. Think of it as a "best of" compilation, or even as a radio DJ's selection of programmed songs. Playlists can be whatever you want (whether based on a mood, theme, etc.) and are simple to create. They're also necessary for a variety of tasks, such as burning CDs and limiting the songs that are shared with other computers.

Creating a playlist

Follow these steps to create a custom playlist:

 Tip *Items can be dragged directly from a CD into a playlist to add them to that playlist while instantly importing the songs into iTunes using the current import settings (in iTunes Preferences).*

1. **Choose File ➪ New Playlist (figure 4.18), or click the + (plus) button in the bottom-left corner of the iTunes window.** This generates a new, empty playlist.

🍎 **iTunes** **File** Edit Controls Visualizer Advanced Window Help

New Playlist	⌘N
New Playlist From Selection	⇧⌘N
New Smart Playlist...	⌥⌘N
Add to Library...	⌘O
Close Window	⌘W
Import...	⇧⌘O
Export Song List...	
Export Library...	
Get Info	⌘I
My Rating	▶
Edit Smart Playlist	
Show Song File	⌘R
Show Current Song	⌘L
Burn Playlist to Disc	
Create an iMix...	
Update Songs on "Chad Fahs's iPod"	
Page Setup...	
Print...	⌘P

4.18 The New Playlist option in the iTunes File menu.

2. **Select your new playlist in the Source list, double-click the name, and type a new name for it.**

3. **Open your iTunes Library by clicking on it at the top of the Source list.**

4. **Choose a song, or multiple songs, that you want to add to your new playlist and drag them onto the playlist in the Source list.**

5. **To delete a song from a playlist, simply click on it and press the Delete key.** The song remains in your library and is only removed from the playlist. You can think of the playlist as a selection of links or aliases that refer to songs in your library.

Tip To open a playlist in its own iTunes window, simply double-click it in the Source list. A new window should pop up containing only those items from the selected playlist.

Tip You can create a playlist quickly by selecting multiple songs in your library. Hold down ⌘/Ctrl to select multiple, noncontiguous items, and then drag the selected songs into the empty space at the bottom of the Source list. A similar technique is discussed in the following section.

Creating a playlist for an album

Creating playlists by selecting several different songs from your entire library is easy to do, but what if you wanted to just create a playlist of an entire album? This feature is particularly useful if you want to burn a CD of an album, because the burn function requires that you start with a playlist. Also, sometimes accessing your favorite albums (especially on an iPod) is easiest if the album is in a playlist.

Follow these steps if you want to instantly turn an album into its own playlist:

1. **Open the iTunes Browser by choosing Edit ⇨ Show Browser or press ⌘/Ctrl+B. See figure 4.19.**

2. **Locate an album that you want to turn into a playlist by navigating down the list in the Browser's Album column (located on the far right of the iTunes window).**

4.19 The Browser in iTunes is a good way to sort music or quickly access an album for turning into a playlist.

3. **Click and drag the album's name from the Browser into the empty space at the bottom of the Source list, located on the left of the iTunes window.** You simply add a new playlist under the last existing playlist in the Source list.

4. **Click once on your new playlist to select it and access it like any other playlist.**

Creating a Smart Playlist

Smart Playlists are playlists that are automatically generated based on an assortment of criteria that you've selected. A Smart Playlist might be composed of songs that belong to a certain genre, have a specific star rating, or fall into some other category. The number of options that can be specified makes these playlists a great organizational and sorting tool, especially for large collections and unique requests. They're also a fun way to create interesting combinations of related tracks. For example, you could quickly create a playlist of your highest ranked music from the 1980s. The combinations are endless.

Follow these steps to generate a Smart Playlist:

1. **Choose File ➪ New Smart Playlist (figure 4.20).** The Smart Playlist dialog box appears.

4.20 The New Smart Playlist option in the iTunes File menu.

2. **Select the Match the following condition option if it isn't already.** Only select this option if you want to specify a specific set of criteria for your playlist. Otherwise, leave it deselected.

3. **Select an option from the first drop-down menu, which begins with the word Artist by default (figure 4.21).** Typical options would include Album, Artist, or Song Name, although you can include many more-obscure items such as Bit Rate, Size, Time, or Year.

4. **In the second drop-down menu, choose the type of operation that you want to apply. Choose from the following: contains, does not contain, is, is not, starts with, or ends with (figure 4.22).**

5. **Enter a keyword or other defining item for the criteria selected in Step 4 in the text field on the far right.** For example, if you chose contains, you might enter **Song Name** and **sky**, which would ask it to find only song names containing the word sky.

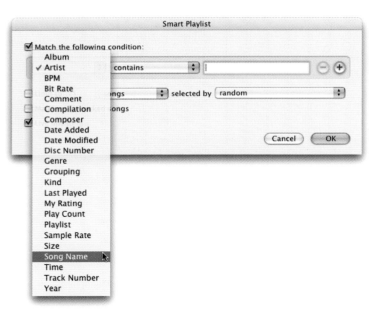

4.21 Choose a set of criteria to use for organizing your Smart Playlist.

6. **Select the Limit to option and enter a number if you want to restrict the number of results that are applied to your playlist.** This may include limiting the Smart Playlist's number of songs, minutes, hours, megabyte requirements, or gigabyte requirements (figure 4.23).

7. **If you chose the Limit to option in Step 6, you can choose a selected by option to determine the way your results are sorted.** Choices include random, album, artist, genre, song name, highest rating, and lowest rating among others as shown in figure 4.24.

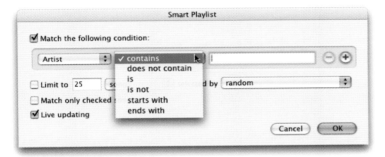

4.22 Select an appropriate operation to apply to your previous criteria and the following text field.

4.23 Limit to options for a Smart Playlist.

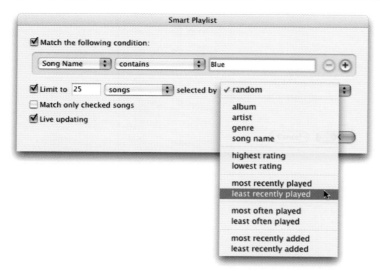

4.24 Selected by options for the Limit to option in a Smart Playlist.

8. **Select Match only checked songs if you want to include only those songs you place a check next to in your library.**

Tip *Unchecking songs is a good way to remove music that you know you don't want as part of a Smart Playlist. Perhaps they're songs from an album you've grown tired of, or a CD that was given to you by a friend. Simply uncheck the box to the left of songs in your library that you don't want to hear as often, and let iTunes sort them out.*

9. **Select Live updating if you want iTunes to check for new songs to update your Smart Playlist with.** As you add new songs to your iTunes library from CDs, the iTunes Music Store, or other sources, your Smart Playlist checks to see whether they might fit the criteria you specified and adds them to your other selections.

10. **When you're finished setting up your Smart Playlist, click OK.** Your Smart Playlist is added to your Source list next to all your other playlists.

Party Shuffle

Party Shuffle is a fun addition to iTunes that allows you to mix music on the fly while a random selection of songs is playing. This is ideal for a party situation where you have music constantly playing yet may want to edit the songs that are playing at any time without stopping the mix.

Follow these steps to perform a Party Shuffle:

1. **Click on the Party Shuffle icon in the Source list (see figure 4.25).**

4.25 The Party Shuffle icon in the iTunes Source list.

2. **Select a Source for your mix from the drop-down menu at the bottom of the iTunes window shown in figure 4.26.** You can choose Library if you want your entire music collection to be used for the shuffle. You can also choose a specific playlist.

3. **Choose the number of recently played and upcoming played songs to display from the Display menus in the lower-right of the iTunes window.** It's especially good to know what songs are coming up, because it gives you more time to edit the mix.

4. **Start your Party Shuffle by clicking the Play button.**

As your Party Shuffle playlist is playing, you can open your Library or another playlist and select a new song, and then drop it onto the Party Shuffle icon in the Source list. After a song is in your Party Shuffle playlist, you can drag it to a new location in the list, or simply leave it at the bottom of the list. At any point you can delete a song, add another, or change the order of songs as desired.

Tip

You can click the Refresh button in the top-right corner of the iTunes window if you want to generate a new, random selection of songs in your Party Shuffle list.

4.26 Options for a Party Shuffle are listed at the bottom of the iTunes window.

Controlling Song Volume

4.27 The iTunes main volume-control slider.

While listening to music played with iTunes, you may change the volume for any songs that are playing. Changes to volume can be applied to all songs or to an individual song quite easily.

Adjusting volume for all songs

Sometimes your entire iTunes listening experience needs a boost in volume. To raise or lower the volume for all songs, drag the volume control slider (located in the upper-left corner of the iTunes window, directly beneath the playback controls) to the right or left (figure 4.27).

4.27 The iTunes main volume-control slider.

If the volume is still too soft or too loud, adjust the volume of your computer's sound through its main system preferences window.

On a Mac, click on the Sound icon in the bar on the upper-right portion of the screen and drag the slider up or down. You can also adjust sound options by opening the Apple menu, selecting System Preferences, and clicking the Sound icon to access additional sound controls (see figure 4.28).

On a PC, the simplest method is to click on the small Sound icon in the lower-right corner of your screen and adjust the volume

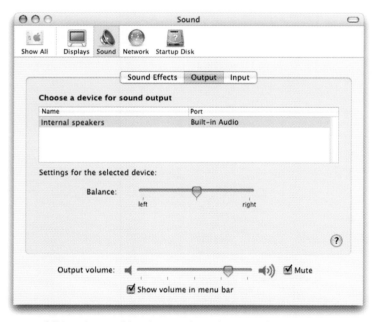

4.28 Additional sound-level controls in the Sound portion of a Mac's System Preferences window.

from there. Additional sound controls on a PC can be accessed through the Control Panel menu or by double-clicking (instead of single-clicking) the sound icon in the lower-right corner of your screen.

Sound Check

Sound Check makes all songs play at the same volume regardless of the original recording level of a song. Follow these steps to make all songs play at the same volume.

1. **Choose iTunes ➭ Preferences.** The iTunes Preferences window opens.

2. **Select the Audio pane in the Preferences window.**

3. **Select the Sound Check option as shown in figure 4.29.**

Adjusting volume for individual songs

All songs are not recorded equal. Some songs are recorded or performed at higher or lower volume levels than others, even from the same artist and on the same album. In order to hear a song at a unique volume level (relative to the master controls for your computer and its recorded level), follow these steps:

1. **Select a song from the Library or a particular playlist by clicking on it.**

2. **Choose File ➭ Get Info or press ⌘/Ctrl+I.** The Info window for the selected song appears (figure 4.30).

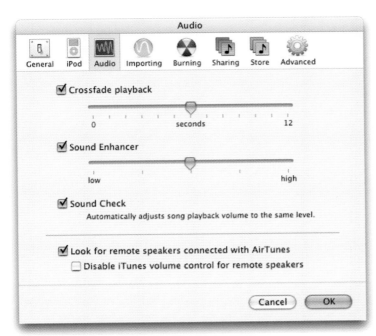

4.29 The Sound Check option makes all songs play at the same volume level.

4.30 The Summary tab in the Info window for a selected song in iTunes.

3. **Click the Options tab in the song's Info window.** You adjust the specific volume for the song here (see figure 4.31).

4. **Drag the volume control slider to adjust the level for the individual song.**

5. **Click OK.** The volume for that song is now set at the level you chose.

 Note *Song volume may also be adjusted in the Equalizer window as described in the next section.*

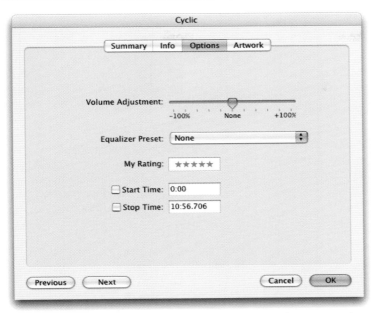

4.31 The Options tab in the Info window includes volume controls.

Adjusting Equalizer Settings

The relative quality of songs changes due to the way the tracks were originally created in the studio or as a result of your sound system's speakers. Some songs were meant to be heavier on the bass, while others require a higher range of frequencies. The option to adjust your listening experience to suit your tastes and the demands of the music is certainly nice.

The ability to customize the high, middle, and low frequencies of your audio is sometimes necessary because different speakers and headphones may be significantly different. At times, such as when listening to music on a laptop, using small speakers, or any setup lacking a wide range of dynamics, adjusting certain frequencies can help significantly to bring your music into an enjoyable audible range. Boosting the bass can

make dance tracks bounce the way they were meant to, while giving more weight to the middle or high frequencies can enhance a violin solo or an opera singer's voice.

iTunes includes several equalizer settings that are specifically tuned to different genres, which can help to enhance the properties of a particular style of music. For example, you might have a track on an album that is in an electronic style, while another is more pop. Selecting the appropriate equalizer preset for that track can bring out its best qualities. Also, iTunes allows you to adjust equalizer settings using a range of sliders, depending on the specific requirements for a track.

Using equalizer presets

Refer to these steps if you want to choose an equalizer preset for a song or group of selected songs:

1. **Choose a song from the Library or a particular playlist by clicking on it.**

2. **Choose File ⇨ Get Info or press ⌘/Ctrl+I.** The Info window appears.

3. **Click on the Options tab in the Info window.**

4. **Click on the Equalizer Preset drop-down menu, and choose a preset from the list.** There are many different genres to choose from (see figure 4.32).

5. **Click OK.**

Making custom equalizer settings

Use the following steps to make custom adjustments to the equalizer settings, rather than using the presets as described in the preceding set of steps:

1. **Click on the Equalizer button (the button with three vertical bars) in the lower-right corner of the iTunes window (figure 4.33).** The Equalizer window opens.

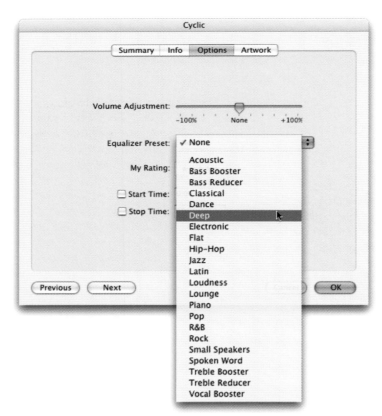

4.32 There are a variety of Equalizer presets for songs in iTunes.

25	☑ Le soleil est près de moi (D...	⊘	3:59	Air	⊘	Le soleil est pr
26	☑ Jynweythek	⊘	2:23	Aphex Twin	⊘	Drukqs
27	☑ Vordhosbn	⊘	4:51	Aphex Twin	⊘	Drukqs

112 songs, 8.8 hours, 499.8 MB

Use the Equalizer to change specific audio frequencies.

4.33 The Equalizer button at the bottom of the iTunes window.

2. **Drag the slider for a particular frequency up or down, which adjusts the volume of that frequency as measured in decibels (dB).** You might also think of a frequency's volume as its strength, with the higher levels representing greater force in the track. The ten frequencies listed horizontally across the Equalizer window represent the equalizer's spectrum. Frequencies on the left denote the low end of the equalizer's spectrum (32 Hz is the lowest), while those on the right represent the highs (16 kHz is the highest).

3. **Raise or lower the Preamp slider if your music is too loud or too soft.** The Preamp slider (at the left of figure 4.34) controls the volume of all frequencies equally. Increasing the Preamp is particularly helpful for increasing the overall levels of a very quiet track.

4.34 The Equalizer window contains a wide range of frequency settings that are controlled by sliders.

4. **Click the close button to close the Equalizer.** If you want to save your settings, choose Make Preset from the Equalizer's pop-up menu before closing the Equalizer as described next.

Saving a custom equalizer preset

After you've made a custom equalizer setting, you can save it and apply it to other songs at any time in the future. Just follow these steps:

1. **Click on the Equalizer button in the lower-right corner of the iTunes window.** The Equalizer window opens.

2. **Make adjustments to frequencies by moving sliders up or down as desired.**

3. **Choose Make Preset from the drop-down menu at the top of the Equalizer window when you are ready to save your settings.** The Make Preset dialog box opens (figure 4.35).

4.35 The Make Preset option in the Equalizer window.

4. **Type a name for your new preset and click OK.** The preset you created can now be accessed through any Equalizer drop-down menu (figure 4.36).

 Tip   *You can delete or rename an existing preset by choosing Edit List from the top of the drop-down menu in the Equalizer window.*

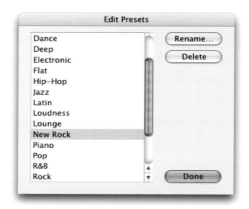

4.36 The Edit List window is accessed through a drop-down menu for Equalizer presets.

Importing Music from a CD

Most iTunes and iPod users are music lovers and likely have a substantial CD collection. A CD collection is often the primary reasons for purchasing an iPod. How often do you consider what it would be like to take an entire music collection with you wherever you go? Importing music from a CD for use on an iPod, or on your computer, is an effortless process with iTunes software. Simply pop a CD into your CD-ROM/DVD-ROM drive and let iTunes work its magic. Of course, you have to make a few decisions about your music files.

The first decision is what format to convert your audio into. Importing an entire CD as uncompressed audio can take up a lot of space on your hard drives — not to mention the fact that transferring and playing uncompressed audio off an iPod can lead to further complications, such as less space for other types of files (particularly when used as a hard drive), reduction of skip protection (because large files monopolize the built-in memory buffer), and occasional hiccups or longer seek times. The solution is to choose from one of the compressed audio formats mentioned at the beginning of this chapter. Ripping audio from a CD and converting it

to AAC or MP3 is ideal for storing files on your computer and transferring them onto an iPod.

Follow these steps to import music from a CD to your Library:

1. **Choose iTunes ⇨ Preferences and click on the General icon.** Make sure you select the appropriate setting in the General pane, as well as having chosen the encoding method you want employed in the Importing pane of the Preferences window.

2. **Choose Import Songs and Eject from the On CD Insert portion of the General window (see figure 4.37).** If you don't want your songs to import automatically when a CD is inserted, change these settings now, or after you're done with the following steps.

Tip

It is usually easiest and most convenient to have iTunes automatically import and eject a CD, because it saves time by automating the entire process of converting your CD collection, without additional clicks. This is particularly helpful if you have a large number of discs to convert.

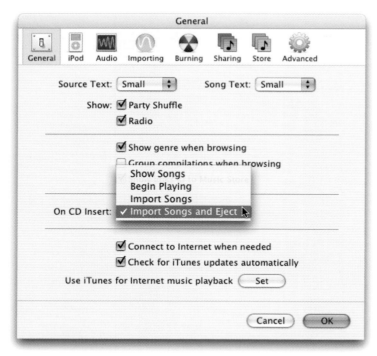

4.37 Automatically importing songs when a CD is inserted into a drive is one of the most popular options for bringing music into iTunes quickly.

3. **Click OK to close the Preferences window.**

4. **Insert a CD into your CD-ROM or DVD-ROM drive.** iTunes automatically begins importing your songs as shown in figure 4.38. It checks an online database for song titles, if you have that option selected (it is, by default), which it automatically applies to your new tracks. This saves a considerable amount of time entering information by hand, which would be tedious, especially for large collections.

5. **If songs don't begin importing automatically, select the songs you want to import by checking the box to the right of a song, and click the Import button in the upper-right corner of the iTunes window (figure 4.39).** Songs are added to your library, and the progress bar lists the amount of time (and speed) that it takes to import the current track.

4.38 iTunes in the process of importing a song.

4.39 The Import button at the top of the iTunes window.

Joining CD tracks

If songs on a CD should be imported without a space of silence in between each track, then you must join them together. Joining creates a single track out of multiple, adjacent tracks; this may be important for the occasional spoken-word or live-music CD.

Although joining tracks can improve the listening experience in these situations, it can also make skipping to individual tracks or navigating quickly through a long recording difficult later on. In general, joining tracks is not usually done, at least not for entire albums. Still, it's a good option to have, and it may be acceptable, particularly for that concert album you may have lying around.

To prevent a gap or silence from occurring between certain tracks, follow these steps:

1. **Make sure the tracks are listed in ascending order (the default for iTunes).** Click on the Song Name column heading and look for an up-turned arrow to its right (figure 4.40). If the songs are not ascending you can click the Song Name column heading a second time to point the arrow downward.

4.40 An upturned arrow indicates that songs are arranged in an ascending order.

Note *Although it's not necessarily intuitive, ascending order simply means songs are listed beginning with track 1, followed by track 2, and so on.*

2. **With the CD inserted into your CD-ROM or DVD-ROM drive, select the adjacent audio tracks that you want to join.** You can hold down the Shift key while clicking on multiple items as shown in figure 4.41.

3. **Choose Advanced ⇨ Join CD Tracks (figure 4.42).** When these songs are imported, they will be joined.

4. **Click the Import button in the top-right corner of the iTunes window to begin importing tracks from your CD without gaps in between.**

4.41 Select adjacent audio tracks that you want to join.

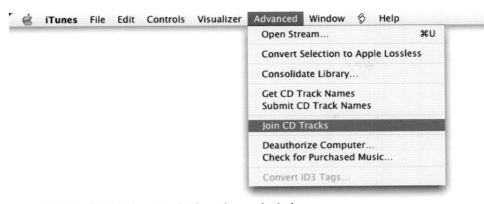

4.42 The Join CD Tracks option in the Advanced window.

Burning Playlists to a CD

Every now and then, you may decide it would be nice to have a copy of your music on a compact disc. Perhaps you want to burn a mix CD of songs for a friend, or (in the case of frequent iTunes Music Store users) you need to back up music you've purchased online. Fortunately, iTunes is able to easily allow burning of your music to a CD. You may even burn a disc or MP3s, which can be played back on some specially equipped CD and DVD players, for many hours of music on a single disc.

To begin, organize the music you want to burn into a playlist, as described earlier in this chapter. After your music is in a playlist, it's simply a matter of making certain your Burn preferences are correct, initiating the Burn function, and inserting a new disc when prompted.

Follow these steps to transfer the music you've added to a playlist onto a CD:

 Note *Playlists containing songs purchased from the iTunes Music Store can only be burned a maximum of seven times.*

1. **Choose iTunes ⇨ Preferences.** The Preferences window opens.

2. **Click the Burning tab.**

3. **Select Maximum Possible for Preferred Speed.** This is the default, but check it nonetheless (see figure 4.43). This setting indicates the speed that your CD burner should use when creating the disc. If your CD burner is rather slow, or if you've been experiencing problems while burning discs at higher speeds in the past (resulting in numerous failed discs), choose a slower setting.

4. **Select the Audio CD button in the Burning tab if you're burning a traditional audio CD.** If you want to create a disc of MP3s for use on a special player (an add-on feature for CD and DVD players that has been appearing in recent years), choose MP3 CD instead (see figure 4.44).

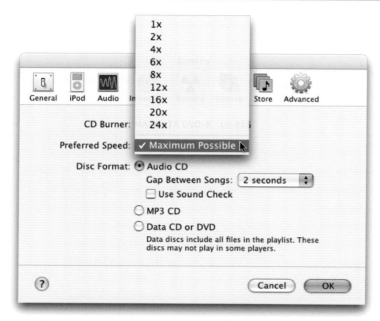

4.43 Burning settings for creating a typical Audio CD from iTunes.

4.44 MP3 CDs are a popular alternative to a traditional audio CD because they can fit several times as many songs on them.

Note *If you choose to create an MP3 CD, just remember that if your songs are in AAC or another compressed format, they will be re-encoded to MP3 and may lose some quality as a result.*

5. **Set the time for the gap between songs.** Although the default of 2 seconds between each song is standard, you can alter the Gap Between Songs setting now, particularly if you're burning a CD of a live concert or spoken-word audio, where you might want to choose None, to eliminate pauses between tracks as much as possible (figure 4.45).

6. **Click OK.**

7. **Select the playlist you created with the songs you want to burn from the Source column on the left side of the iTunes window.**

8. **Click the Burn Disc button in the upper-right corner of the iTunes window to initiate the burning process (see figure 4.46).**

9. **Insert a blank CD-R disc when prompted, and then sit back and let iTunes burn your audio or MP3 CD.**

4.45 The default gap of 2 seconds between songs is typical, although you may choose a different duration.

4.46 The Burn Disc button at the top of the iTunes window.

Tip

To avoid an annoying pop-up message informing you that a blank disc has been inserted into your computer, make sure you click the Burn Disc button before inserting a CD-R.

Converting Songs to Another Format

Regardless of which format your music begins in, you can usually convert it to another, more appropriate format in iTunes. With iTunes, you can easily convert songs from one format to another, such as an AIFF file to AAC, or (if you're using the Windows version of iTunes) a non-DRMed WMA file to MP3. This feature comes in handy when you've acquired music in uncompressed formats and you want to compress them to fit on an iPod or to take up less space on your hard drive.

Follow these steps to convert a song from one file format to another:

1. **Choose iTunes ➪ Preferences to set up iTunes for the format conversion you want to make happen.** The Preferences window opens.

2. **Click the Importing tab.**

3. **In the Import Using drop-down menu, select an encoding format that you want to convert a song to.** For example, if you want to convert your audio to a compressed format, choose AAC Encoder or MP3 Encoder from the list shown in figure 4.47.

4. **Check your settings by looking in the details window.** The defaults are usually fine, but you can make any necessary changes by clicking on the Custom option in the Setting drop-down menu.

5. **Click OK to accept these settings and close the Preferences window.**

6. **Select songs in your iTunes window by clicking on them.**

7. **Choose Advanced ⇨ Convert Selection to AAC (whichever format you have selected in the Preferences window should appear here) as shown in figure 4.48.** The conversion process begins immediately.

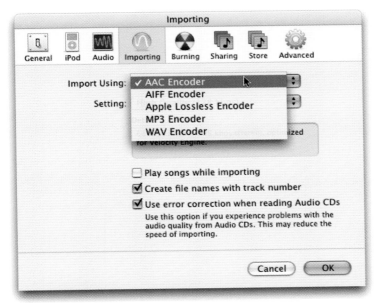

4.47 There are multiple encoding formats to choose from in the Importing options of iTunes Preferences window.

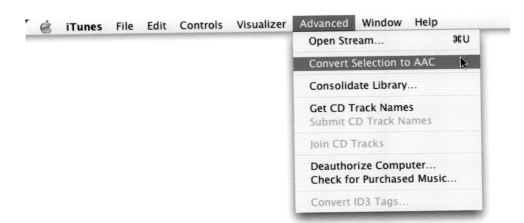

4.48 The Convert Selection to AAC option in the Advanced menu.

Consolidating Audio Files

Depending on how you began using iTunes to import and play back your music and other audio, you may have files in your iTunes library that are floating around your hard drive, or even on multiple drives in different locations. Keeping track of all this audio can be a real hassle, which is why consolidating all your music into a central location, where it can be easily accessed using iTunes software, is usually best.

Consolidating is important if you want to make sure that you don't keep multiple copies of the same files, which take up extra space, or if you decide at some point to move or remove files, which can accidentally break the link to items in your iTunes library. After these files are consolidated, you can easily back them up to another

hard drive or disc for safekeeping, or even transfer them to another machine. In any case, keeping your computer tidy is always a good idea, and consolidating your audio files to a single location is a great way to do this.

Follow these steps to organize all your audio files by copying them into your iTunes music library:

1. **Choose Advanced ⇨ Consolidate Library from the iTunes menu (see figure 4.49).** This takes all your music files in iTunes and copies them to your iTunes Music folder. The files that were already in your iTunes Music folder are not affected.

2. **When you're ready to accept the terms of the consolidate option, click Consolidate as shown in figure 4.50.**

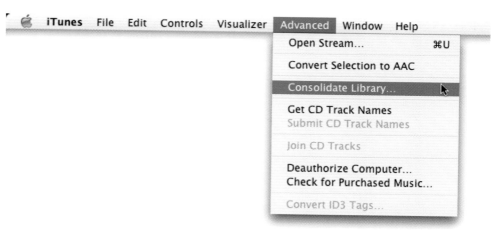

4.49 The Consolidate Library option in the Advanced menu.

4.50 Choose Consolidate to move your audio files into the iTunes folder.

Note *All the files in your library that were outside your iTunes Music folder are copied there without removing them from their original location. When all your music is consolidated, you may want to delete the extra files.*

Printing Covers for Mix CDs

Assuming you used the steps outlined earlier to burn a CD from an iTunes playlist, producing a cover to place inside the case with your disc is often a nice touch (especially when you're trying to remember what music is on a disc).

Because recordable CDs are so cheap these days, you can easily burn dozens, if not hundreds, of discs and let them lie around your house without knowing what's on them. Adding a label or writing on the disc itself is the first step to identifying your media. This is something that iTunes leaves up to you.

Many decent labeling applications are out there, including those that may ship with third-party CD and DVD burning software such as Roxio's Toast and Easy CD Creator. Where iTunes can help you is with the creation of simple booklets that include

pictures and track information for the CDs you've created. By simply selecting a playlist or your library, you can print entire master lists of your audio (like a spreadsheet of your music collection), or quickly produce inserts for your cases.

The following steps illustrate how to quickly create a printed case insert for the CDs you burn from iTunes:

1. **Select the playlist you created for the CD you have burned or intend to burn.** You can also select your Library instead of a playlist if you want to produce a master list of your music for reference purposes.

2. **Choose File ➪ Print to open the Print window (figure 4.51).**

3. **In the Print window, select one of the Print option buttons: CD jewel case insert, Song listing, or Album listing (figure 4.52).** If you are producing an insert for a CD case, the first option is most appropriate. However, you may also choose to print out a master list of the songs in your selected playlist or iTunes Library. This produces a sheet of all song, album, track length, and artist information, as seen in the individual columns of your iTunes window. For the Song Listing option, you may even choose to include User Ratings, Dates Played, or Custom to determine what information is displayed. If the Album Listing option is selected, a thumbnail of your album is displayed on the left, with artist, song, and track lengths listed to the right.

4.51 The Print option in the File menu.

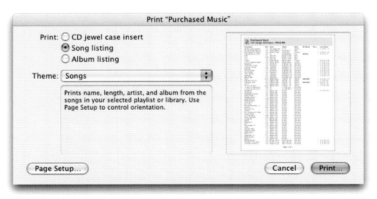

4.52 Choose print options in the Print window.

4. **If CD Jewel Case Insert was selected as the Print option, select one of the following options from the drop-down list:**

   • **Text Only and Text Only (Black & White).** For the standard Text Only option, only the text for songs is printed against a colored background (the default color is blue) as shown in figure 4.53. This is a simple and elegant choice, particularly if you don't have album artwork for your tracks. If Text Only (Black & White) is selected, the list is printed against a white background with black text.

   • **Mosaic and Mosaic (Black & White).** Mosaic creates a color collage of all the album covers associated with the songs in your playlist, which prints out on the front and back of the CD insert as shown in figure 4.54. If Mosaic (Black & White) is selected, everything looks the same, except the artwork is black-and-white against a white background.

   • **White Mosaic.** Similar in every way to an ordinary mosaic, except a white line separates the album art and it's printed against a white background (see figure 4.55).

4.53 The Text Only jewel case insert printing option is selected.

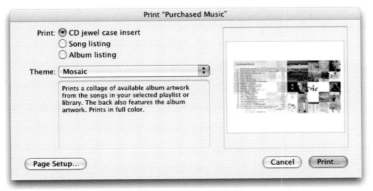

4.54 The Mosaic jewel case insert printing option is selected.

- **Single Cover.** This is generally the nicest choice if burning a single album of music as shown in figure 4.56. The artwork that is associated with the currently selected song is displayed on the front and back of the insert in full color.

- **Single side (Black & White).** For a no-frills, single card insert for a CD case (without the typical front and back covers, and so on), this option may be the most appropriate (see figure 4.57). All of your songs are listed on one side in black-and-white.

- **Large playlist (Black & White).** If you have a lot of music in the playlist you're burning (for example, if you're burning a disc of MP3s, where you can fit around 100 tracks on a CD), this may be the option for you (see figure 4.58). Large playlists are printed on the insert by starting on the front cover and continuing on the back. Nothing fancy here, just all the track information you might need printed in glorious black-and-white.

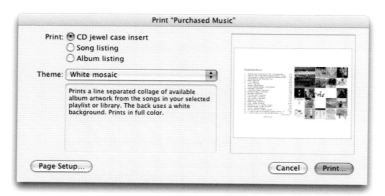

4.55 The White Mosaic jewel case insert printing option is selected.

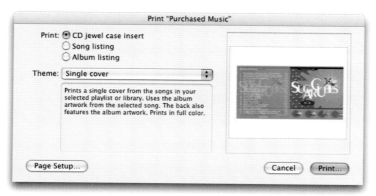

4.56 The Single Cover jewel case insert printing option is selected.

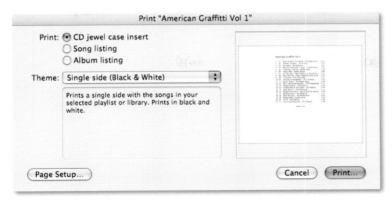

4.57 The Single side (Black & White) jewel case insert printing option is selected.

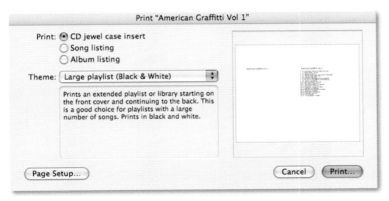

4.58 The Large playlist (Black & White) jewel case insert printing option is selected.

5. **Click Print to initiate the printing process.** At this point, you would print as you ordinarily do using your computer.

If you're using a Mac, you may choose Save As PDF during the final Print step (see figure 4.59). This is a convenient option if you want to keep a digital reference file of your music on your hard drive, or if you want to e-mail a list of song and album information to a friend or colleague.

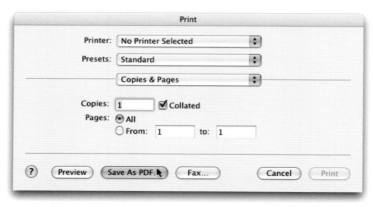

4.59 Saving as a PDF is a convenient method for keeping a page for later reference or printing.

Visualizing Your Music

iTunes includes a Visualizer, which produces random visuals to complement music that is playing. With Visualizer turned on, abstract shapes and colorful designs appear to dance to the sounds produced by iTunes. This is a fun feature for parties or for just relaxing with the lights turned down low. Now, you can produce your own light show at home without traveling to your local planetarium. So throw on some Pink Floyd and see what patterns emerge.

Follow these steps to activate Visualizer:

1. **Select a song or a playlist in the iTunes window, and then press the Play button or double-click the song to make it play.**

2. **Click on the Visualizer button in the lower-right corner of the iTunes window (figure 4.60).** The Visualizer button is to the left of the Eject button and looks like a flower.

4.60 The Visualizer button at the bottom of the iTunes window looks like a flower.

3. **Choose Visualizer from the menu bar and select an appropriate frame size (figure 4.61).** The options for size include Small, Medium, Large, and Full Screen. Slower computers may need a smaller frame size to play back smoothly, while most computers will work fine even with images in full-screen mode, which is the ideal way to view these images. The iTunes window displays the Visualizer.

4. **Click on the Options button for Visualizer in the upper-right corner of the iTunes window (figure 4.62).** The Visualize Options dialog box appears.

5. **Select options for viewing the Visualizer (figure 4.63).** Choose the following:

   - **Display frame rate.** This tells the Visualizer to display the frame rate in the upper-left corner.

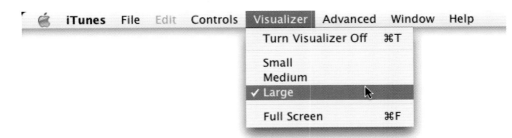

4.61 Choose a frame size from the Visualizer menu.

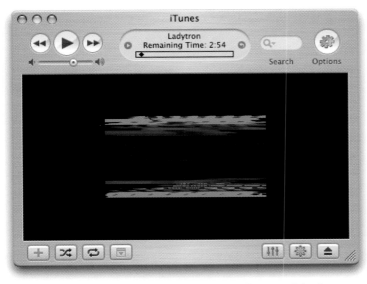

4.62 The Options button for the Visualizer at the top of the iTunes window.

- **Cap frame rate at 30 fps.** Some computers can display images even faster than 30 fps, but may eat up system resources and experience intermittent lags in playback.

- **Always display song info.** The information for songs appears automatically in the bottom-left corner of the iTunes window but may disappear without this option checked.

- **Use OpenGL.** This option tells the iTunes Visualizer to use the OpenGL graphics library to draw its content.

- **Faster but rougher display.** This option smoothes out the motion on a slower machine.

6. **Click OK.** Your song plays with the Visualizer in action (see figure 4.64).

7. **When you finish using the Visualizer, click the Visualizer button again to turn it off.** If you're in full-screen mode, you may have to press the Escape key first to return to your desktop.

4.63 The Visualizer's Options menu.

Tip

Online you can find a number of plug-ins that add functionality to the default Visualizer in iTunes. Google the phrase **iTunes Visualizer plug-ins** and see what you find. You can find numerous other Visualizers or even create your own, if you're adventurous enough to delve into Apple's developer kit. When you locate some new effects plug-ins, you can place them in your iTunes Plug-ins folder, restart the software, and then check out the new shapes and patterns.

4.64 A typical Visualizer experience includes colorful moving lines and simple shapes.

iTunes Radio

One of the really nice extra features of iTunes is its ability to access streaming-radio broadcasts over the Internet. No longer do you have to open a separate player window on your computer to access some of your favorite radio stations. With this free, easy-to-use service, you can simply open your iTunes software, choose a station that you want to listen to, and turn up the volume.

Whether you're at work or just passing time at home, the option to receive radio broadcasts through your computer is very convenient — you don't have to install an antenna or remain limited by the programming on your local radio airwaves. You have a number of music and talk categories to choose from — there are enough options to satisfy

the majority of listeners. International broadcasts are some of the most unique options to choose from, because they're not easy to access any other way.

Use these steps to access free radio broadcasts through your iTunes software:

1. **Make certain that you have a working Internet connection and your computer is online.**

2. **Click the Radio icon in the Source list, located on the left side of the iTunes window (see figure 4.65).** A list of radio categories appears. Typical categories include Alt/Modern Rock, Ambient, Blues, Classic Rock, Classical, Country, Electronica, International, and others.

4.65 The Radio button is located in the Source list.

3. **Click on one of the triangles to the left of a category you're interested in (see figure 4.66).** A list of associated radio stations should appear as choices beneath the selected category. There may be dozens of radio stations to choose from in a given category.

4. **Locate a station that you want to listen to.** Make certain that its bit rate matches the capabilities of your Internet connection. Some stations have multiple bit rates to accommodate all listeners (see figure 4.67). If you use a cable or DSL modem, no station should be a problem. However, if you're using a dial-up Internet connection, make sure you look for bit rates at or below 56 Kbps.

4.66 There are a variety of genre categories in iTunes Internet Radio.

5. **Double-click on a radio station in the list to access it.** Audio should begin playing almost immediately (depending on the station's Web site) after you've selected a radio station. Notice that information for the music you're listening to is usually displayed scrolling across the top of the main iTunes display (see figure 4.68).

Occasionally, network problems stall playback of a particular station, which requires iTunes to rebuffer the stream it's trying to receive (see figure 4.69). This can cause a pause or complete stop of playback. Usually, streams can be rebuffered and are fine, although sometimes a bad connection cannot be fixed. In this case, try back later to see if the station is up and running again.

4.67 Some stations broadcast at multiple bit rates to accommodate a wide range of users.

4.68 Information for the audio from a radio station is displayed at the top of the iTunes window.

4.69 Occasionally, connection with a radio station fail and need to be buffered again.

Using iTunes with AirPort Express and AirTunes

AirPort Express is a hardware device sold by Apple that allows you to gain Internet access anywhere that there is a WiFi connection. It also allows you to stream music wirelessly to any location in your house that is within range of your AirPort Base Station using a feature called AirTunes.

Apple's AirPort Express makes it possible to create a link between your computer and stereo, actually bypassing your iPod (see figure 4.70). After your network has been set up and your AirPort Express device has been installed in an outlet near your stereo, you can launch iTunes and make a few settings that enable music to begin streaming through the airwaves.

Courtesy of Apple

4.70 AirPort Express is able to stream music wirelessly throughout your home.

Follow these steps to set up iTunes for use with AirTunes, a feature of the AirPort Express device:

1. **Make sure that your AirPort Express device is plugged into a wall outlet and that speakers are properly connected to it.** Staying within range of your AirPort Base Station is important.

2. **Choose iTunes ⇨ Preferences and select the Audio pane in the Preferences window.**

3. **Select the Look for remote speakers connected with AirTunes option.** If AirPort Express is functioning properly, you should see your remote speakers as an option in a drop-down menu at the bottom of the iTunes window.

4. **Choose your speakers from the menu.** Volume can be controlled through iTunes.

 Tip *You can turn off the option to control volume remotely for speakers that are connected to an AirPort Express device (in case you want your stereo's receiver to control volume better) by choosing the Disable iTunes Volume Control for Remote Speakers option in the Audio pane of the Preferences window.*

Sharing Music over a Network

If your computer is connected to a network with other computers, you can share your iTunes music with those other computers. This is a convenient option for a workplace environment where people are dispersed throughout an office yet would like to access each other's music. With sharing activated, you can view and play someone else's songs, although you can't copy these songs to your own library or playlist, and you can't burn discs with this music. Also, if music was purchased from the iTunes Music Store, it cannot be shared unless the other computers are authorized to play it (up to five computers may be authorized to share your iTunes Music Store purchases). Additionally, spoken-word files downloaded from Audible.com are in a slightly different, more-strictly-guarded format, which cannot be shared over a network. Just remember to

deactivate sharing if you're on a network and you don't want others to see what's in your iTunes music library.

 Note *In order for others to view your shared music, iTunes must remain open on your computer.*

Follow these steps to allow other people on your network to share your music:

1. **Choose iTunes ⇨ Preferences to open the Preferences window.**

2. **Click on the Sharing pane at the top of the Preferences window (figure 4.71).**

4.71 Sharing options in the Preferences window.

3. **Select the Share my music option.** Additional options become available (see figure 4.71).

4. **Select Share entire library or Share selected playlists, depending on what music you want to make accessible.**

5. **If you choose to share selected playlists, check the boxes next to all the playlists you want to include as part of your shared music.** If there are any personal playlists you don't want to share, now is the time to make sure they're deselected (see figure 4.72).

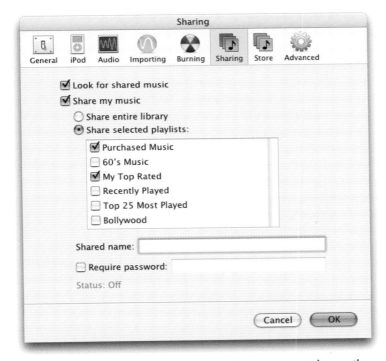

4.72 With the Share Selected Playlists option, you must choose the playlists that you want to include.

6. **Type a name in the Shared name field to identify your computer (see figure 4.73).** You can be clever here or simply use the default name that identifies your computer on the network.

7. **If you want to require a password to log in (so that only a chosen few may access your**

music), **check the Require password option and type a series of letters and numbers to the field of the right (see figure 4.74).**

8. **Click OK when you're done, to accept your changes and close the Preferences window.**

4.73 Type a name for your shared identity.

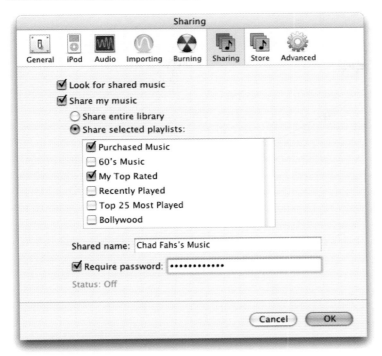

4.74 You can include a password to protect your shared music from unwanted visitors on a network.

iTunes Music Store

I f you have been collecting music for several years, you probably have a large collection of CDs that are taking up a lot of shelf space. iTunes makes it possible to convert those discs into digital files that can be stored and played back on your computer's hard drive or your portable iPod digital music player. Although this has been the primary use of an iPod for several years now (and continues to be an important use of the device), it is now possible to purchase your music as a download only, which bypasses the shiny plastic discs known as CDs and replaces them with something that takes up no additional physical space at all — except the space already taken up by your hard drive or the size of your iPod. The iTunes Music Store is the revolutionary service introduced by Apple in 2003, which lets you download individual songs or entire albums over the Internet. This chapter discusses the iTunes Music Store, the services it offers, and the functionality it adds to the iTunes software.

About iTunes Music Store

As of this writing, the iTunes Music Store has passed a major milestone. In the past two years (it opened in April of 2003), over 300 million songs have been downloaded and purchased from the iTunes Music Store. The success of the iTunes Music Store demonstrates the viability of downloaded music and the growing acceptance of the technology among consumers. Of course, the business of legally downloaded music, whether with iTunes or other services like Napster 2.0, continues to evolve and flourish due to the popularity of the iPod.

5.1 The iTunes Music Store is a one-stop shop for music lovers who live online, or those who just buy music there.

In order to use the iTunes Music Store, you must first have a computer with the iTunes software installed. (The iTunes Music Store is accessed through the iTunes software and not through a Web browser.) You also need to have a credit card and a billing address in the country whose iTunes Music Store you are using. Apple continues to add more iTunes Music Stores for specific countries, including Canada, the United Kingdom, and Japan, to name a few.

Tip

The iTunes Music Store is accessed through the Source list in the iTunes software. If you don't see Music Store in the Source list, choose iTunes — Preferences, click the Store tab, and check the Show iTunes Music Store box.

iTunes Promotions

In recent years, Apple engaged in promotional deals with Pepsi to provide free song downloads from the iTunes Music Store. In this particular promotion (which may take place once again by the time you read this), Pepsi drinkers were given a one in three chance to find a bottle cap with a code underneath that enabled them to download one free song from the iTunes Music Store. The campaign required new users to sign up for the service (an ID and credit card information are required for new users), resulting in new enrollees in the service and the creation of future iTunes Music Store addicts. Another example of a promotional arrangement with the iTunes Music Store includes Apple's agreement to provide AOL users direct links to the online store, giving AOL's membership better access for music purchases and instant one-click buying power. Information on the most recent iTunes Music Store promotions can be found by going to www.itunes.com.

Opening a Store Account

When you try to purchase a song or album through the iTunes Music Store, you're prompted for your account information (login and password). If this is your first time using the service, you may need to enter some billing data. All that is needed to purchase music from the iTunes Music Store is a valid credit card and a little bit of time to fill out some information. If you're already a .Mac member, you can sign in with your .Mac user ID. In addition, AOL members can use their AOL screen name to log in.

> **Note** *The computer that you use to sign up to the iTunes Music Store is important. Whichever computer you first sign up with is automatically added to the list of authorized machines that are able to play songs that you buy using your new account. This authorization can be changed at a later time if you want to switch it to another computer.*

The following steps demonstrate how to open a new account for the iTunes Music Store.

1. **Open the iTunes application.** Make certain that you're connected to the Internet (preferably with a high-speed connection, such as DSL or cable) before proceeding beyond this step.

2. **Select Music Store from the Source list in iTunes.**

3. **Click the Sign In button to the right of Account, located in the top-right corner of the screen.**

4. **If you haven't used the iTunes Music Store, click the Create New Account button on the login screen that appears.** If you already have an account, Apple ID, or AOL screen name that you want to use, click Sign In.

5.2 Click the Sign In button to initiate the login process or to open a new account.

Sign In to download music from the iTunes Music Store
To create an Apple Account, click Create New Account.

(Create New Account)

If you have an Apple Account (from the Apple Store or .Mac, for example), enter your Apple ID and password. Otherwise, if you are an AOL member, enter your AOL screen name and password.

Apple ID:

Example: steve@mac.com

Password:

(Forgot Password?)

(Cancel) (Sign In)

5.3 Click Create New Account if you're a new user, or enter your Apple ID or AOL screen name to log in to your existing account.

5. **Enter an e-mail address and password that you want to use.**

6. **Proceed to the next page and enter all the credit card and billing information that is requested.**

7. **Click the Done button when you're finished.** If your credit card and account information were processed correctly, you should be taken to the iTunes Music Store, and the e-mail address you provided should be displayed in the upper-right corner of the iTunes window (next to Account). You're now able to begin browsing and making purchases in the iTunes Music Store!

Finding and Buying Music

If you're familiar with navigating Web pages, browsing catalogs, and making purchases online, then finding songs and buying music

in the iTunes Music Store should be no problem. In fact, the navigation is similar to the iTunes application itself (not surprising as this is where you're viewing the Music Store content). When you locate a song you think you might like (or if you're simply curious about an artist you've never heard), you can preview a 30-second sample of the song before you buy, which is also a great way to find new music.

Exploring the iTunes Music Store involves moving back and forth through sequences of pages. At any point, you can click the Home button to return to the main page (where you began your search), or you can go back to another page you've already visited. In addition to being a good place to start your search, the main home page lists new releases, current favorites, and special promotions. On the left side of this screen, you should see more criteria for browsing music. Choose a genre, such as Electronic, to view its own special main page with information on relevant new releases in that category.

The following steps demonstrate how to browse for songs in the iTunes Music Store.

1. **To access the iTunes Music Store, click on its icon in the iTunes application Source list (labeled Music Store).** It is located on the left side of the main iTunes window.

2. **To locate a song in the iTunes Music Store, type in a word into the Search field and press Return on your keyboard.** The Search field is located in the top-right corner of the window. Search results are presented instantly.

Tip

You can also browse categories quickly by pressing the Browse button, choosing a genre, and scrolling up and down the list of artists and titles. Navigating the iTunes Music Store is a little different from viewing a site in your Web browser, although many of the same principles apply. Because the store is not simply a Web page, but a part of the iTunes application itself, it can utilize different sets of buttons and navigation features, some of which you might not ordinarily encounter.

5.4 You can find music on iTunes by entering an artist's name, song title, or other keyword.

5.5 In addition to finding music with the search field, you can press the Browse button to peruse songs in long lists, which are generally divided according to genre or other criteria.

3. **Scroll through the list of song titles to view the search results.** Notice that there are columns for the type of information you would ordinarily find in iTunes, such as Song Name, Time, Artist, and Album. You can sort these lists accordingly by clicking on the column heading at the top of each list. For example, if you've received a large number of search results, you can click the column heading labeled Artist to view songs grouped alphabetically by a band or performer.

4. **When you've located a song you want to preview, double-click the song name to listen to the 30-second clip.**

5. **If you decide to purchase a song, click the Buy Song button in the Price column.** You can also choose to purchase an entire album (usually at a discount from purchasing songs individually), by double-clicking the album name in the browser list and then clicking on the Buy Album button at the top of the page that appears.

When you purchase a song or album, that music is downloaded to your computer and placed in the Source list's Purchased Music playlist.

Tip

If you like a particular artist and want to have easy access to his or her iTunes Music Store information in the future (in case you want to look for new music), you can activate buttons that appear next to a song title and instantly take you to that artist's page on the store site. To turn on the arrows that appear next to a song, choose iTunes ➪ Preferences, select the General tab, and turn on the Show Links to Music Store option.

1-Click Feature

The iTunes Music Store includes the option to buy music with the special 1-Click feature. Activating the 1-Click feature allows you to click a Buy Song or Buy Album button and instantly purchase and download music (it will prompt you for your account login the first time during a session). This could be an expensive option, indeed, if you're prone to impulse purchases. You may be familiar with a similar option on Web sites like Amazon.com. To easily activate or deactivate this feature, choose iTunes ➪ Preferences, click the Store tab, and check (or uncheck) the Buy and Download Using 1-Click box.

5.6 Purchasing with 1-Click makes buying music quick and easy.

Authorizing and Deauthorizing a Computer

Songs purchased from the iTunes Music Store include a form of Digital Rights Management (DRM), which prevents songs from being copied and played on more than the predetermined number or type of devices. This is part of Apple's Fair Play Framework, and it's how Apple managed to get music labels to agree to offer their artists' music through the iTunes Music Store service. Although some form of copy protection may be necessary if the online music business is to flourish, this leaves consumers (the ones buying the music) with an interesting problem. After purchasing a song, you might assume that you own it and, therefore, can use it on whatever device you want, or even share the songs with your family and friends. The reality is that the songs downloaded from the iTunes Music Store (available in a special AAC audio format designed by Apple) are only playable on iTunes or iPod devices, and even these devices may have limitations and restrictions imposed on them.

The following list includes restrictions for songs purchased from the iTunes Music Store.

✦ **Songs are playable on up to five different computers.** However, each computer must be authorized using your iTunes Music Store account information. For example, when you attempt to play a song that you purchased on your home computer while on a friend's computer, you're prompted for your account name and password.

✦ **You can play a song you purchased on any number of iPod devices.** This is because the iPod must first be connected to an authorized computer before it can download the song.

✦ **Using the iTunes software, you can easily burn CDs of songs you have purchased.** Burning songs to a CD is an important way to back up data and music you've paid for. However, if you're burning a playlist that contains a song purchased through the iTunes Music Store, that playlist can only be burned a maximum of seven times.

You can manually authorize another computer to play your iTunes Music Store purchases. This might be important if you listen to your songs on more than one computer (for example, a computer at home and another at work). In addition, a computer can be deauthorized, in case you purchase a new machine, decide to sell an old computer, or otherwise want to revoke listening privileges from a roommate or sibling. Make sure that you're connected to the Internet before attempting to authorize or deauthorize a computer.

Follow these steps to authorize a computer to play your iTunes Music Store purchases:

1. **Open the iTunes software.**

2. **Attempt to play a song for which this computer is not authorized.** An Authorize Computer dialog box appears — enter your account information.

Follow these steps to deauthorize a computer from playing your iTunes Music Store purchases:

1. **Open the iTunes software.**

2. **Choose Advanced ⇨ Deauthorize Computer.** Select the deauthorization option (iTunes Music Store or Audible.com) you desire in the Deauthorize Computer dialog box that appears.

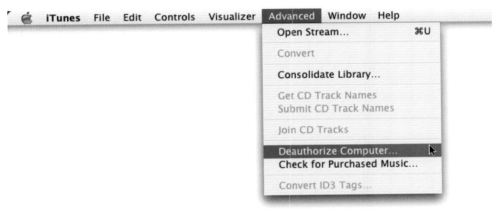

5.7 The option to deauthorize a computer is located in the Advanced menu.

Publishing an iMix

If you've created a great playlist (or mix of songs), you can share it with the world using the iMix feature in iTunes and the iTunes Music Store. An iMix is a list of songs, which may include notes about the music you've chosen, just like a celebrity playlist, and is searchable by anyone with iTunes and Internet access (a large number of potential viewers, considering the popularity of iTunes and the iPod). This feature helps store shoppers find new music based on their interests. Perhaps you've just put the finishing touches on your ultimate party

mix. Now you can publish your mix online and send an e-mail to your friends letting them know where to check it out. The iTunes Music Store will notify you of which songs in your submission are available— only the available songs appear in an iMix when it is published.

Note A link to the iMixes page is located on the left side of the main page in the iTunes Music Store. You can quickly search the available iMixes by entering text in the Search For field and selecting a criteria, such as iMix Name, Artist Name, Album Name, Song Name, or All.

5.8 Due to the large, and active, iPod and iTunes community, searching iMixes and finding lists of songs for just about every artist, genre, or theme is easy.

Follow these steps to create an iMix, which you can publish on the iTunes Music Store:

1. **Open the iTunes application.**

2. **Create a new playlist by selecting File ⇨ New Playlist.** An untitled playlist appears in your Source list, with the name selected for ease of editing.

3. **Type an appropriate name for your playlist.** Playlists published as an iMix are searchable by their titles, in addition to the usual criteria for song, album, and artist names, so be specific to make finding the iMix easier. For example,

"My Favorite Tom Waits Songs," or try something that includes the name of the artist or genre it's a part of, such as "Best Emo of 2005." You can name the iMix whatever you like, although finding it may be difficult if its title is not descriptive.

4. **Click on Library in the iTunes Source list, locate songs you want others to see in your iMix, and drag them onto the new playlist in the Source list.**

5. **When you're finished arranging your playlist, choose File ⇨ Create an iMix.**

5.9 The option to Create an iMix is located in the File menu.

6. **Sign into your iTunes Music Store account to publish your iMix.** The Music Store takes over the song list pane, displaying a header where you can give your iMix a title and description (the playlist name is the default title) and a list of the songs in the playlist available through the iTunes Music Store.

7. **When you're ready to officially add your iMix to the iTunes Music Store, click Publish.**

After publishing an iMix, iTunes prompts you to notify your friends that you've published a new iMix. Click the Tell A Friend button to send an e-mail announcement.

You can rate an iMix by checking the appropriate star rating, from 1 to 5, located at the top of the iMix page. Highly rated iMixes (based on average ratings) are featured more prominently in the iTunes Music Store.

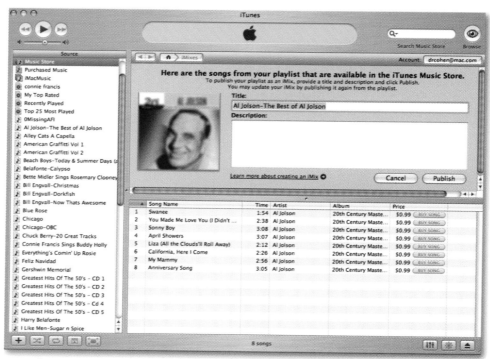

5.10 The Music Store's iMix page with your header and songlist.

5.11 Clicking Publish uploads your new iMix.

iTunes Link Marker

Another interesting feature of the iTunes Music Store is the ability to add iTunes Link Markers to your Web pages. Using the iTunes Link Markers, you can connect users who visit your site to specific songs, albums, or artists in the iTunes Music Store. These links provide a convenient way to promote the music you enjoy and to give fellow Web surfers, customers, or people just browsing your Web site, blog, or home page, with more information on your favorite bands. To find out more about link markers, and to generate the necessary code for a link, visit www.itunes.com.

Spoken Audio Content and Audible.com

Books and periodicals don't have to be published on paper or as e-books (PDF files and so forth). Bookstores, Amazon.com, and numerous other book dealers, even Wal-Mart and Target, have discovered that a significant portion of the public enjoy the convenience and experience of listening to their favorite books, magazines, newspapers or radio programming where and when they like.

You might be taking a long drive and want to see what Tom Clancy or Stephen King's latest bestseller can do to make the miles pass more quickly, but you know that the Highway Patrol (or other law enforcement agency) would look askance if you were to have the novel perched on your steering wheel while cruising down the Interstate. Or you may want to listen to your favorite radio show without re-arranging your schedule. Enter the audiobook and Audible, with its wealth of spoken audio content, ranging from best-selling audiobooks, to the New York Times, Wall Street Journal and the New Yorker, to This American Life, The Bob Edwards Show, Charlie Rose, Fresh Air and Opie & Anthony, to name a few. Spoken audio content is a popular option for use with iTunes and your iPod.

> **Tip**
> *Purchasing via the iTMS is definitely very convenient, but you're almost guaranteed to be paying as much or more for your titles by doing so. In addition to taking advantage of specials and incentive offers at Audible's site, you can also sign up for subscription plans that can save you money if you're a frequent shopper.*

From iTunes' introduction, Audible.com has enjoyed an exclusive relationship with Apple as the purveyor of spoken audio content, and magazines for use in iTunes (and on your iPod). You can purchase Audible.com titles through the Audiobook section of the iTunes Music Store or directly from Audible's Web site (www.audible.com). Purchases made via the iTMS download immediately into your iTunes Library. The same is true if you make your purchase from Audible; Audible's DownloadManager software will import your downloaded file into your iTunes Library for you (available at www.audible.com/software). On the Macintosh platform iTunes works with purchases made from Audible with no additional software.

> **Note** Purchases from iTunes are not protected against lost or deletion. If you buy a title from iTunes and your hard drive crashes you have to buy the title again. Purchases from audible.com can be downloaded again and again at no extra charge.

Regardless of method, purchases of Audible.com titles give you an Audible file (extension .aa if purchased from Audible and extension .m4b if purchased from the iTMS). These files employ DRM, requiring authorization to play on a computer, just as iTMS song purchases do. In fact, a virtually identical dialog box appears asking you to authorize a computer to play Audible titles when you first attempt to do so. Similarly, there is a radio button for Audible

content in the Deauthorize Computer dialog box (Advanced ➪ Deauthorize Computer). Spoken audio content purchased from the iTMS employ Apple's FairPlay DRM and are treated like any other iTMS-purchased material.

> **Cross-Reference** For more information about DRM and how it works, see Chapter 7.

> **Tip** Some books you purchase from Audible.com may be offered in a choice of formats. The iPod recognizes only Audible 2, 3, and 4 formats, something to remember when offered this choice. Format 2 has the greatest compression, allowing you to store more books in the same space, but with a corresponding loss in sound quality. Format 3 is the format intended to provide the best quality/compression balance for spoken word recordings. Format 4 is really MP3 in a .aa wrapper so as to allow bookmarks in iTunes and on the iPod, but is twice as large as Format 3.

There are some additional restrictions related to using Audible.com-purchased files in iTunes and on your iPod, the most significant is that you can only place files from a maximum of two Audible accounts on your iPod, as indicated in figure 5.12. If you want to add content from a third account, you must remove the content from one of the other two accounts. Similarly, you can only authenticate three computers (the iPod doesn't count as one of the computers) to play the files from an Audible account.

If you stop listening to an Audible file and then reopen it later, it starts playing from the point you stopped rather than the beginning. You can rewind if you want to revert to an earlier point or restart the playback. This feature is called a *bookmark*.

Most Audible files contain chapter markers. You can skip from chapter to chapter in iTunes by pressing Shift+⌘+→ (Shift+Ctrl+→) to move forward or Shift+⌘+←

(Shift+Ctrl+←) to move backward. Additionally, when a file with chapter markers is playing in iTunes, the display area contains a chapter marker icon that functions as a popup menu, allowing you to choose a chapter.

 Note *The iPod shuffle does not recognize chapter marks, but iPods, iPod minis, and iPod photos do, treating each chapter as a separate track.*

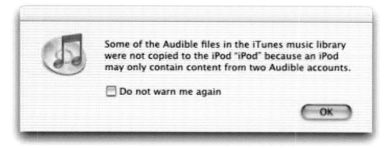

5.12 You can only have Audible content from two accounts on an iPod.

Getting the Most Out of the iPod

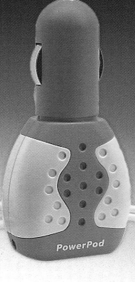

iPod Accessories

Because of the iPod's phenomenal success, it was only a matter of time before an entire industry emerged around the iPod. Currently, accessories are available to meet nearly every use for the world's most popular digital music player. The assortment of devices to augment a stock iPod continue to grow and will no doubt have increased by the time you read this. In fact, the number of useful, fun, curious, and stylish add-ons that can be purchased could fill an entire book in itself.

In this chapter, I cover the main categories of accessories, giving a few examples of the products available in each. This chapter should provide a starting point for you if you're interested in expanding the capabilities of your iPod. It might also inspire you to create a few of your own accessories, such as a custom case.

Earphones and Headphones

An iPod, or any portable listening device for that matter, is only as good as the earphones or headphones that are connected to it. In addition to the standard earbuds included with each new iPod, you can purchase a plethora of personal listening devices from a wide range of manufacturers. The following are a few categories for small headphones (or earphones, take your pick), which are perfect for mobile users.

Earbuds

Although the earbuds that come with each iPod are fine for many users, they're more biased toward the high-end frequencies and tend to have less bass and a narrower range of sound than most separately purchased in-ear earphones/headphones above $40. Most earbuds that you can purchase separately are inexpensive and relatively comfortable (because they sit outside the ear), although they don't create a seal in the ear or produce the results of in-ear designs.

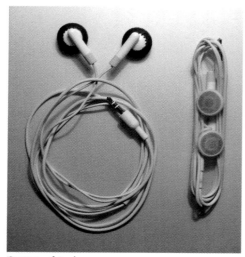

Courtesy of Apple

6.1 Apple's white earbuds are the signature of an iPod user.

In-ear

As the name implies, these earphones are inserted into the ear canal, making for a much snugger and, therefore, more "sound-tight" fit. The majority of high-quality earphones use an in-ear design, starting with Apple's own iPod In-Ear Headphones, which can be purchased from the Apple Store. In-ear headphones differ depending on the tightness of fit, the amount of sound they're built to keep out, and the range of frequencies they can reproduce. The best types of in-ear headphones are sound-isolating.

> **Note** *Bluetooth-enabled headphones are the next wave of listening devices. Hewlett Packard, Griffin, Belkin, and Macally are a few of the companies that are already producing wireless headphone solutions, although the next version of Bluetooth technology (Bluetooth 2.0) will likely bring more and possibly even an entry from Apple.*

In-ear, noise-isolating headphones are essential for the best quality sound in noisy locations, such as when traveling or using your iPod outdoors. Etymotic Research makes excellent earphones of this type, which have become an industry standard for musicians and others who demand the best sound in a small package. Of course, like any other digital device, you pay a bit more for the technology. The Etymotic ER-6i Isolator earphones have a list price around $149, while the high-end Etymotic ER4S lists for about $330. Shure makes good isolating earphones between $119 (Shure E2C) and $500 (Shure E5C, with excellent bass response). Sony also makes good isolating earphones, such as the MDR-EX70, MDR-EX71s, and MDR-EX81, which list for around $59.

larger portable speaker systems, such as the Bose SoundDock, JBL OnStage, and Tivoli iPal, make a difference in sound quality and can provide enough volume for most rooms in your house. Many of these devices, such as the Bose SoundDock, provide a dock for your iPod, which passes the music to the speakers without your having to connect or disconnect cables. As an added bonus, the built-in dock charges your iPod while you listen to your music.

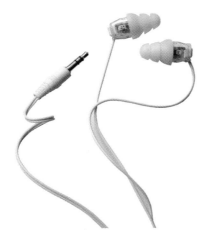

Courtesy of Etymotic

6.2 Etymotic's ER-6i Isolator earphones are an excellent alternative to the Apple earphones.

iPod Speaker Systems

Choosing a set of speakers to complement your iPod is essential if you want the convenience of listening to your iPod at home without headphones. Of course, with the correct cables, you can plug your iPod directly into an existing stereo system or listen to audio through speakers hooked up to your computer. However, speaker systems designed specifically for the iPod make docking, charging, and listening to your music easier — they also look great in just about any room of your home.

In the category of portable speaker systems, there are the JBL On Tours, Pacific Rim Technologies Cube Travel Speakers, Macally PodWave, and Altec Lansing inMotion, to name a few. Unfortunately, the sound quality of portable — and especially ultra-portable — devices are often what you would expect from a speaker that size. The

Courtesy of Bose

6.3 The Bose SoundDock produces great sound in a small package (dock included).

Courtesy of JBL

6.4 The JBL OnStage is another speaker system with built-in dock.

iPod Remote Controls

Some of the earlier versions of the iPod came with a remote control as standard equipment. Currently, the only way to get a remote is to purchase one separately. (Apple has been cutting back on the frills to keep prices low.) Apple's remote control is positioned between the iPod and the headphones, which are plugged into the remote-control unit. The remote-control unit is then plugged into the remote and headphone jacks on the iPod. The remote provides the requisite controls, such as play/pause, next, previous, volume up, and volume down.

In addition to wired remotes, you may also purchase wireless devices to control your iPod. The basic principle is that a receiver unit is attached to the top of the iPod and a separate remote-control unit (that looks like a miniature TV remote) is used to control it by sending a signal to the receiver. Units such as Ten Technology's NaviPod are based on infrared (IR) principles and must

Courtesy of Griffin

6.5 The Griffin AirClick is an RF remote control that works through walls, unlike line-of-sight infrared controls and receivers.

be aimed directly at your iPod in order for it to work. Griffin Technology, one of the most popular iPod accessory companies, is shipping an AirClick remote control, which uses RF technology to control the iPod from up to 60 feet away. Because it uses RF signals, not line-of-sight infrared beams, you can control an iPod through walls and around corners from another room.

FM Transmitters and Car Adapters

Listening to your iPod with headphones is fine for walking to the office, working out, or passing time at the airport, but it isn't the best solution when driving in your car, which (with a decent set of speakers installed) is already the ideal personal listening environment.

> **Caution** *In some states, listening to headphones while operating a vehicle is actually illegal. Make sure you know the law in your area before using headphones while driving.*

Unfortunately, most cars are not equipped with a built-in audio jack, or a car auxiliary port, for connecting with your iPod. (Some higher-end carmakers, such as BMW, Mercedes Benz, and Volkswagen are the exception, with vehicles that are specially equipped for use with an iPod.) For the rest of us, there are FM transmitters and car adapters for sending an iPod's music through nearby speaker systems. In fact, the use of a transmitter is not limited to the car — you can use any radio with a tuner.

By turning the iPod into its own FM radio station, you can listen to an iPod through virtually any stereo, wirelessly. Simply tune the stereo to a channel that matches the channel being broadcast by the iPod's FM transmitter. The most noticeable drawback to this type of listening is the difference in quality when compared with ordinary stereo performance, because the signal is susceptible to interference and usually needs to be within a few feet of the receiver for acceptable results. If you find the results distracting (with static and broken signals for example), you may want to consider paying to have a custom line-in jack installed in your car, or purchasing a cassette adapter (if your car is equipped with a cassette deck).

Griffin Technology makes a very convenient device called iTrip, which is small, looks great with your iPod, and is easy to use. The iTrip plugs into the headphone and remote-control jacks on the top of your iPod (separate models are available for full-size iPods and the iPod mini) and transmits audio to a receiver that is tuned to a specific frequency. (Out of the box, this channel is usually the lowest on the dial, such as 87.9, although that can be changed with software that comes with the device.) All power for the iTrip is drawn from the iPod's battery, so you don't have to worry about opening the device or replacing old batteries. The only drawback to the lack of batteries is a slightly weaker signal than models with their own batteries.

Courtesy of Griffin

6.6 The Griffin iTrip is an FM transmitter that is small, stylish, and easy to use right out of the box.

Belkin offers a device called the TuneCast, which works in much the same way as the iTrip; however two AAA batteries are required, which helps to boost the signal. Xtreme Mac also makes FM transmitters for iPods, including a model for the iPod shuffle, which is extremely small, plugs into a cigarette lighter, and allows a user to tune to a specific frequency on the device itself. (The built-in LCD screen makes matching the AirPlay's frequency to your car radio easier than using radio-station playlists and special software, like Griffin's iTrip.)

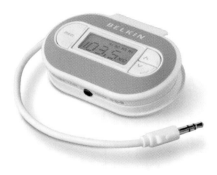

Courtesy of Belkin

6.7 The Belkin TuneCast FM transmitter allows you to easily change frequencies to match the ideal station on your radio.

Monster, a company known for its stereo cables and home-theater connections for audiophiles and videophiles, produces wireless FM transmitters that are built into car

adapters, which power and recharge your iPod as you listen to music. The iCar Wireless Plus also comes with a small screen that shows the station you're tuned to and allows you to easily change frequencies until you find the best reception.

Cassette adapters can be used in place of a transmitter, and they produce better results, because they aren't susceptible to the interference that results from sending a signal through the air. Some cassette adapters even add additional features. For example, the Griffin SmartDeck allows you to navigate your iPod through your cassette deck's playback controls. Griffin, Belkin, Monster, Sony, and many other companies produce cassette adapters that can be used with an iPod. You may already have a suitable cassette adapter if you've used your car's cassette deck with a portable CD player.

Courtesy of Griffin

6.8 Cassette adapters are the preferred method for playing your iPod through your car's stereo if you don't have a direct audio line-in but you do have a cassette deck.

iPod Cables

Most of the companies mentioned here also produce a variety of audio and video cables to meet your iPod and iPod photo needs. Monster is an example of a company that specializes in cables, although they tend to be a little pricier than the type of cables you would find at Radio Shack. Typically, users are often looking for a way to connect their iPods to home stereos. The easiest way to accomplish this is to use a cable that starts with the headphone jack connection on your iPod (a ⅛-inch, male stereo connector) and splits into two RCA (left and right, male) connectors that plug into your stereo's receiver. Monster sells the iCable, which does just that, although you can find similar cables in the TV or audio section of any retail store. Griffin, Belkin, and others also sell this type of cable.

Another popular type of audio connection is a splitter, which allows you to share your headphone jack with two pairs of headphones. This can be useful for airplane trips with a companion, or hanging out with friends on a train or at the beach. Belkin and many other companies make headphone splitters.

iPod Power Sources

Although an iPod is typically charged in its Dock or through the FireWire/USB 2.0 cable when connected to a computer, other accessories can help extend the battery life or charge an iPod while on the road. If you're going camping or planning another long trip where you won't have access to an AC outlet, you might consider bringing one of these devices along.

Car chargers are a good way to recharge your iPod's battery when on a road trip, or even while driving to work. Using a car charger also means you don't have to drain the iPod's battery while listening to music in your vehicle (such as when using the FM transmitters or car adapters mentioned earlier). Griffin produces a PowerPod car charger for iPods that plugs into the cigarette lighter, and Belkin sells an Auto Kit that interfaces well with the Belkin TuneCast (or cassette adapter) through the use of an audio-out jack. Monster also sells a variety of car chargers, including models with built-in FM transmitters.

Griffin sells a separate battery backup for the iPod and iPod mini called TuneJuice, which plugs into the Dock connector on the bottom

6.9 Splitters allow you to share your music with others by creating two headphone jacks from one.

Courtesy of Griffin
6.10 Car chargers are a great way to power and recharge your iPod while on the go.

of the iPod and provides up to eight additional hours of play time (four hours if the iPod's battery is already drained). A 9-volt battery is inserted in the TuneJuice to provide the additional power, which is great for traveling, because you can purchase 9-volt batteries just about anywhere. Belkin also makes portable power sources for the iPod, such as the Backup Battery Pack and the TunePower rechargeable battery pack. The TunePower rechargeable battery pack provides an additional eight to ten hours of playtime to your iPod. It's also very slim, attaches to the back of your iPod or iPod mini using special sleeves, and includes a power-level indicator.

 Note *A new category of power-producing devices for the iPod use solar technology. Solio is one company that is shipping solar-powered chargers that are compact (fit in a pocket) and versatile. You can also use it to charge other devices you might carry with you on a sunny day, such as mobile phones and PDAs.*

Courtesy of Belkin

6.11 Battery backups add power when you need it most.

iPod Docks and Stands

Unfortunately, Apple has pretty much done away with including Docks with iPods. If you want to easily add audio outputs to your iPod, sync you music, and access your files without connecting and disconnecting cables, or access the video-slideshow features of iPod photo, then you need to purchase one of these $29 (for the iPod shuffle Dock) to $39 cradles.

Although most iPod owners use an Apple Dock or the built-in dock on a portable speaker system to hold their iPods, you can purchase special stands to securely hold your player in a variety of situations. For example, Griffin makes an iSqueez holder for the car, which sits in a cup holder and securely holds your iPod while you drive (perfect for use with the iTrip or another FM transmitter). Belkin also makes a car holder for the iPod called TuneDok. Manufacturers including Thought Out (iPed), Power Support, and DVforge also produce alternative stands for the iPod.

iPod Cases and Attire

The largest explosion of iPod accessories is in the cases category. Cases are easy to produce, offer a wide range of designer styles and uses, and provide protection for a variety of daily situations and environmental conditions.

The list of companies producing their own cases is long. A few include Marware, iSkin, Agent 18, Xtreme Mac, Incase, Casemandu, Sumo, Kate Spade, Miyavix, Power Support, and many others. This list does not even come close to scratching the surface of available iPod protectors. There are also waterproof iPod cases, such as OtterBox.

Although not a case exactly, armbands are another type of functional iPod transporter. Of course, these are most practically utilized by the iPod mini and iPod shuffle, which are the right size and weight to be strapped to an appendage. (The iPod shuffle has the added advantage of skip-proof flash RAM.) If you're a jogger or biker, or you simply enjoy wearing your iPod while you exercise at the gym, an armband may be just what you need.

In addition to cases and armbands, iPods are also covered in the clothes department. For example, Burton makes specially designed jackets that feature built-in controls for the iPod on the sleeve. Other companies are also creating handbags and other urban attire that include a special space for an iPod. A company called ScotteVest even sells a jacket with solar panels attached, which can be used to charge your iPod (or any other portable USB device).

Recently, Apple got into the game with its own iPod socks, which are just that — knit socks in a range of five colors. These socks can hold your iPod and protect it from scratches, especially when it's sitting in your pocket or bag, although they're of little use for hard impacts or sharp surfaces. There is a certain novelty (and cuteness) factor with the socks, which cost more than the socks you wear on your feet (iPod socks sell for $29.99 for a set of five). In general, they're probably best as an additional sleeve around another case.

Courtesy of Apple

6.12 Apple's iPod socks keep your iPod warm and safe from minor scratches and dirt.

Special Tips and Techniques

Although deceptively simple on the outside, an iPod can do many things that it was not necessarily designed to do. Anyone willing to spend a little extra time with one of these devices will realize that it is more flexible and fun than a basic digital music player or a viewer for carrying a collection of photos. By delving a little deeper into the world of the iPod and its related products, you can emerge with some helpful and otherwise interesting information at your fingertips. In this chapter, I cover some special tips and techniques that are designed to get you thinking about how to better manage and utilize your favorite portable companion.

iPod Media Management

Now that you have your entire music collection with its thousands of songs on a device small enough to fit in your pocket, what do you do next? Learning how to manage all that music is a good start. In fact, it isn't until you've become familiar with the traditional workings of an iPod and iTunes that you start to question if certain tasks could be accomplished better or with less frustration.

Finding and deleting duplicate songs

When you've been using an iPod and the iTunes software for a while, it's likely that, at some point, you might accidentally (or knowingly) import a song or an entire album more than once. For example, you might purchase an album that includes a copy of a song available on a different CD, or you may have copied your music off another computer or a friend's mix CD. Whatever the reason for having duplicates of your music, you can quickly track down those extra copies and remove them from your iTunes Library. Removing duplicate audio files conserves space on a hard drive, including your iPod, and leaves more room for additional music and data storage.

Follow these steps to locate and remove duplicate songs from your iTunes Library:

1. **Select your iTunes Library or a specific playlist in the Source list.**

2. **Choose Edit ➪ Show Duplicate Songs.** Any songs with the same name and either the same artist or album should be displayed. By looking at the properties of the songs (length, and so forth), you can determine whether they're actually duplicates or just a variations with similar names.

3. **Click once on the song you want to remove.** You can Shift+click to select multiple sequential songs for removal or ⌘/Ctrl+click to select multiple non-contiguous songs for removal.

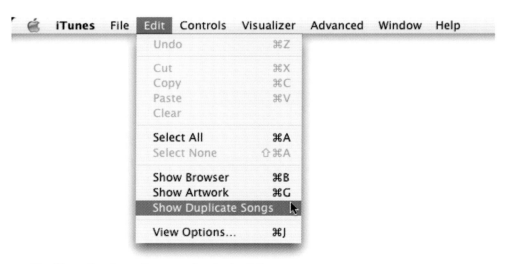

7.1 The Show Duplicate Songs option in the Edit menu.

4. **Press the Delete key to remove the song.**

5. **When you're asked "Are you sure you want to remove the selected items from the list?" click Yes.** References to any songs that were selected are removed from the Library or playlist you were in.

6. **When you're asked whether you want to delete the song from your hard drive, click Yes.** This immediately (and irretrievably) removes the offending file from your iTunes Music folder.

Using songs authorized for another computer

One of the real frustrations of iPod owners who use the iTunes Music Store is that they're limited in the ways they can transfer or use their music. Any songs that you purchase may only be used on the computer you bought them on, or on a select number of computers (five, to be exact) that are authorized to play back the music.

You can deauthorize a computer to play a song and then reauthorize another machine if you run into the maximum-number threshold. Additionally, you can circumvent the digital rights management (DRM) software in your AAC files by burning an audio

7.2 Removing songs from a list.

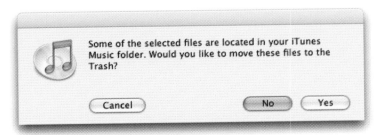

7.3 The last step before songs are removed from your hard drive.

CD or your music and then re-importing the files as unprotected AACs, as documented by Apple. This can be a hassle if you have a lot of music, because you have to burn multiple CDs. Also, any songs that are burned and then re-imported lose a little bit of quality, due to another round of compression applied by the AAC or MP3 encoder.

Importing an AAC file into iMovie and then exporting may also do the trick, although quality is lost with this method as well. Of course, users online post new methods for circumventing DRM. For example, a hacker recently discovered a way to remove DRM when purchasing music from the iTunes Music Store.

In this section, I first outline how to deauthorize one computer so another can access your music. I also suggest an alternate method for circumventing DRM by burning music to a CD and re-importing.

Deauthorizing a computer

Use these steps to deauthorize a computer so another computer may use your shared music:

1. **Make sure your computer is connected to the Internet.**

2. **Choose Advanced ⇨ Deauthorize Computer.** The Deauthorize Computer dialog box appears.

3. **Select Deauthorize Computer for Music Store Account.** If you have downloaded Audible files (spoken work and audio books), then you can choose the second option, Deauthorize Computer for Audible Account.

4. **Click OK.** After you've made your decision, you will be prompted for your account information to confirm the deauthorization.

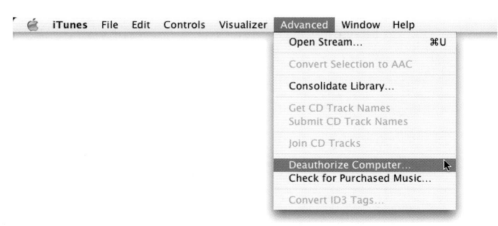

7.4 The Deauthorize Computer command in the Advanced menu.

7.5 Choose the type of purchased music you want to deauthorize for this computer.

Removing DRM

The following steps outline how to remove digital rights management from an AAC file by copying it to an audio CD and then re-importing it into iTunes. Although this is not a recommended step, because it adds additional compression and removes track information, I'm listing it here as the only Apple-acknowledged solution for those who want to freely distribute their music to other computers they own, or to use files in multimedia projects.

1. **Create a playlist containing the music you want to remove the DRM from.** For example, you might select your entire Purchased Music playlist from the Source list.

2. **Choose iTunes ➪ Preferences, and select the Burning pane in the Preferences window.**

3. **Select Audio CD as your Disc Format.**

4. **Click OK to close the Preferences window.**

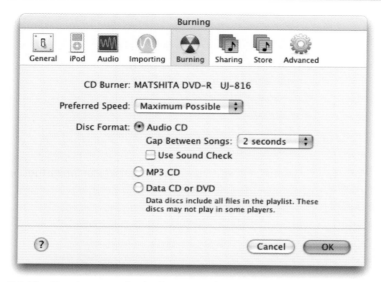

7.6 The Burning pane in the iTunes Preferences window.

Note You can only burn your purchased audio files a maximum of seven times.

5. **Click the Burn Disc button in the top-right corner of the iTunes window.**

6. **Insert a blank CD-R when prompted to do so.**

7. **When the CD is finished burning, open the newly created CD (you can eject it and reinsert it if you prefer) and select all of your songs.** Your songs are now in an AIFF or WAV format and all DRM is removed. Hang on to these discs as a backup of your purchased music.

8. **Make certain your import settings are correct in iTunes Preferences, and then click the Import button in the top-right corner of the iTunes window.** You may also have the Import Songs and Eject option activated in your Preferences window, which eliminates the need to import manually.

Accessing and copying hidden files on an iPod

If you've ever accessed the iPod's disk mode for manually managing songs and copying notes or other data files to the device, you've probably wondered where all your music files are located. When you open the device as a hard drive on your computer, only a few folders are visible (Calendar, Contacts, Notes), although none of them contain your music. This is Apple's way of reminding you not to illegally copy or transfer music.

So, what if you wanted to copy your music (legally, of course) directly off your iPod and onto a computer? If you're on a Mac, you can either download a special tool (such as TinkerTool) to access hidden files, or you can get your hands dirty and break open the Terminal application. Terminal is an application that allows you to access the Unix command line, or *shell,* which allows you to access the powerful Unix features of the OS X operating system. On a PC, accessing these hidden files is easier, and does not require a special utility. Shareware and freeware applications can accomplish this process for you if you would rather make the process transparent. (I prefer to use tools or separate applications for this task as a last resort.) Methods for finding and copying these hidden files are listed here for both systems.

Follow these steps to access and copy hidden files on a Mac without resorting to a separate third-party application (if you aren't interested in learning Terminal, you might consider an option like TinkerTool or PodManager):

1. **Make sure your iPod is connected to your computer and disk mode is enabled.**

2. **Open the Terminal application, which is located in the Utilities folder inside your Applications directory** (`<boot drive>/ Applications/Utilities`)**.**

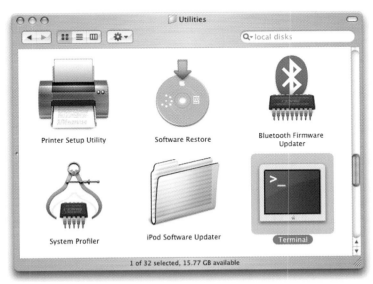

7.7 The Terminal application in Mac OS X is located in the Utilities folder.

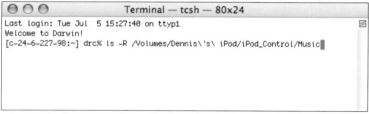

```
 ⊖ ⊝ ⊘              Terminal — tcsh — 80x24
Last login: Tue Jul  5 15:27:40 on ttyp1
Welcome to Darwin!
[c-24-6-227-98:~] drc% ls -R /Volumes/Dennis\'s\ iPod/iPod_Control/Music▮
```

7.8 Terminal commands to display a list of songs on an iPod.

3. **With Terminal open, type** ls -R /Volumes/[insert your iPod's name here]/iPod_Control/Music **(substituting [insert your iPod's name here] with the name of your device).** Depending on which version of OS X you are on (Apple has been fixing this find feature), your songs may be displayed in the Terminal. Be aware that if your iPod's name includes any spaces or punctuation, you need to escape those special characters by preceding them with a backslash (\).

4. **To copy your files from the iPod to a location on your hard drive, type** cp -R /Volumes/[insert your iPod's name here]/iPod\ _Control/Music/ ~/Music/ iPodCopy/ **(substituting [insert your iPod's name here] with the name of your device).** This command copies the entire music folder from an iPod onto your hard drive. The last part of the command determines which directory it is placed inside (in this example, a folder called iPodCopy inside your Music directory, although you can change the location to something more appropriate if you like). You can also use standard copy commands inside Terminal (the cp command in Unix) to copy individual songs. If you're a Mac user interested in the inner workings of your machine, or computers in

general, I would highly recommend learning more about how to use Unix, which can open up a whole new world of possibilities.

Caution *Remember to escape (insert a backslash) before any spaces or special characters in your iPod's name. Similarly, make certain that you have enough free disk space on your destination volume for the entire contents of your iPod Library, because the* cp -R *command will attempt to copy everything in your iPod's Music directory to your hard disk.*

Follow these steps to access hidden files on a PC.

1. **Make sure your iPod is connected to your computer and disk mode is enabled.**

2. **Right-click on your iPod, either on your desktop or in the My Computer Windows Explorer window.**

3. **Choose Tools ⇨ Folder Options.** The Folder Options dialog box appears.

4. **Select the View tab.**

5. **Under Hidden Files and Folders, check the Show Hidden Files and Folders option.**

6. **Click Apply to make the hidden music files visible.** You can now access the iPod's music files directly, which are located inside the iPod_Control folder within a series of subfolders labeled with letters and numbers.

7. **To copy songs or your entire music directory, drag-and-drop files or copy and paste items into a new location on your hard drive, just as you would other types of files.**

Backing up your music Library to DVD

A large majority of music collections span hundreds, if not thousands, of CDs. When these CDs are imported into iTunes, they're usually converted to a highly compressed format like AAC or MP3 to save space and make it possible to store all this music on a single iPod device. Even an iPod mini, at anywhere from 4GB to 6GB (or more), can hold a very substantial collection of over 1,000 songs.

The time it takes to import all that music (not to mention the wear and tear on your computer's CD-ROM/DVD-ROM drive) is enough to make you not want to do it a second time. Backing up your collection is a good idea and highly recommended, particularly for songs purchased from the iTunes Music Store, which are irreplaceable. Having a backup on a hard drive is one good method for keeping your music data safeguarded against drive failure or accidental erasure. Keeping another copy on a recordable DVD is also a good plan, because these discs are small, take up little space, and hold a considerable amount of compressed music. If anything goes wrong with your

iPod or the hard drive where your iTunes library is stored, you can simply pull out the DVD with your music backup and copy it onto your computer again. You can also share it more easily with others this way, or transfer copies of your music to a different computer.

Perhaps you have a computer at work and at home. Bringing a DVD (or multiple DVDs) with your entire collection of songs makes it simple to update the iTunes library on a different computer. Ultimately, the main benefit to backing up to DVD is to keep your music investment, and the time it took to import your music, safe. The piece of mind that comes with having copies of your files is definitely worth the small investment of a couple dollars for discs.

Follow these steps to make a backup of your iTunes Library on DVD using Mac Finder or Windows Explorer:

1. **If you're on a Mac, open the Music/iTunes folder in your home directory. If you're on a PC, open the My Documents/My Music folder.** Assuming that you've been using the Copy files to iTunes Music Folder when adding to library option in the iTunes Preferences window, all of your music files should be contained within these subfolders.

2. **Drag-and-drop all the files and folders listed here onto a blank DVD-R (or DVD+R) disc.** The simplest way to back up your files is to copy the entire iTunes folder. The iTunes Music Library files contain information about your songs and playlists, so keeping them with your music is a good idea.

7.9 Files in the iTunes folder.

3. **Burn your DVD using the built-in disc-burning option in Mac OS X and Windows XP, or use a third-party application, such as Roxio's Toast or Easy CD Creator to make the disc for you.** Control-clicking on Mac, or right-clicking on Windows, should bring up a burn option for your disc, which includes finishing off the disc so that it can be read easily by another computer (although you might not be able to copy any more files onto it after it's done).

7.10 Toast is an alternate application for burning CDs and DVDs on the Mac.

Follow these steps to make a backup of your iTunes music library on a DVD using iTunes to do the burning for you:

1. **Create a new playlist in the iTunes Source list and add any songs to it that you want to back up onto CD or DVD.**

2. **Choose iTunes ⇨ Preferences and click on the Burning pane in the Preferences window.**

3. **Select the Data CD or DVD option for the Disc Format.**

4. **Click OK to accept the change and close the Preferences window.**

5. **Click the Burn Disc button in the top-right corner of the iTunes window.**

6. **Insert a blank DVD when prompted.** iTunes backs up your files to disc, although it does not recompress files like burning an audio CD (or, if you started with AAC, like an MP3 CD might).

7.11 Options in the Burning pane of the iTunes Preferences window with Data CD or DVD selected.

Working with Text on Your iPod

While you no doubt think of audio when you think of the iPod, sound is not the only way in which the iPod communicates. As described elsewhere, you can keep calendar and contact information on your iPod, employing it as a read-only PDA. As an extension to this textual communication, you have a Notes directory on the iPod that allows you to retrieve text messages up to 4KB in size. Enterprising individuals have found many ways to exploit the text retrieval and display capabilities and the following discussion touches on a couple of the more inventive or useful ways.

Reading audiobooks on your iPod

Downloading audiobooks from sites like Audible.com is a great option for keeping up on your "reading" while on the commute to work or traveling. Although listening to your books with an iPod is the preferred method, you can use the Notes feature to carry books in the form of simple text documents.

Although not exactly a traditional read – the iPod's screen is not really suited to this sort of thing with its limited size – it can be useful for short stories, poetry, or when trying to cram for a literature exam while eating lunch. Copy the text you want to read on your iPod into a new text document. If your files are too large (greater than 4K in size), break them apart into separate text files, or locate a shareware application or script online that can do this for you (see the section on AppleScripts in a later part of this chapter). By including links, as described in the following section, you can also link note files to each other.

It's not perfect for creating or reading long documents, but note files on an iPod make the e-book a reality for a wide range of users. Perhaps better support will appear in future iPod releases.

 Note *Notes on an iPod are limited to 4KB. Any additional text that exceeds the 4KB limit is cut off from the bottom of the file.*

7.12 The iPod's Notes folder, accessed through disk mode, is able to hold files for books and other documents put in the text format.

 Note *An iPod can hold a maximum of 1,000 notes.*

Creating links and HTML in note files

Note files can be a very useful feature for keeping track of to-do lists, as well as carrying presentations, short books, and articles wherever you go. With a Links feature, you can turn iPod notes into miniature hypertext documents, just like navigating pages on the Web.

Understanding basic HTML

In addition to being able to recognize text, an iPod can utilize very basic HTML (Hypertext Markup Language) tags. It helps if you've had some prior experience with Web languages, but HTML is probably the simplest computer language to master. Fortunately for new users, the iPod's HTML support is rudimentary by comparison to its use on the Web and easy to pick up. Unfortunately for experienced users, a few of the normal principles of HTML, such as the paragraph tag creating an extra space, don't always work as expected.

Here's a list of basic HTML tags that you can add to your Notes:

✦ `<TITLE> </TITLE>` This tag creates a title at the top of the document, which is a good identifier of the text contained inside (does not appear in the main body of the document).

✦ `<p> </p>` A paragraph tag identifies a block of text as separate from another (comes at the opening and closing of a paragraph).

✦ `<br>` Break tags create a line break that adds space between lines of text. Adding multiple break tags creates more spaces between lines. For example, to create a full line of empty space between text, add two break tags in a row, such as `<br><br>` (similar to using two carriage returns on a typewriter or hitting Enter twice on a word processor).

✦ `<a href=" ">` `<a>` Hyperlinks are denoted by this tag, shown here with a space for the link it is pointing to. Any text in between these opening and closing tags is underlined to indicate that you

may click on the text to jump to another page. In terms of construction, a link is created by placing the linked to page inside the quotation marks. For example, `<a href="Note2.txt">My Second Note Page</a>` is how a typical link is created.

Every HTML tag must have an opening (before the linked text) and corresponding closing tag. An opening tag, such as `<p>`, comes before the text you want to affect, while the closing tag, such as `</p>`, always comes after. As long as you know how to make the opening tag, creating a closing tag is usually a matter of adding a `/` symbol in front of the other tag. Break tags, `<br>`, are one of the few exceptions.

 Note *The iPod cannot display styled text, such as bold or italic.*

Adding links to a note file

Now that you've seen a few HTML tags and what they mean, it's time to jump right in and create a note file that uses a few of them. Using the basic form covered in this section, you can modify and play with the HTML until it's suitable for other, more detailed (and interesting) documents.

Follow these steps to create a note file with links and add it to your iPod:

1. **Open TextEdit on a Mac or Notes on a PC.** If you're using TextEdit on a Mac, make sure to choose Format ⇨ Make Plain Text to remove the Rich Text features that do not work for the HTML document. When the document is properly configured, you should see a `.txt` extension at the top of the page.

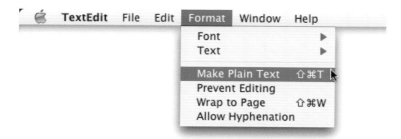

7.13 Text Edit in Plain Text mode is ideal for creating notes.

2. **Create a simple note with HTML, such as the following example:**

```
<TITLE>My First Note
Page</TITLE>
Welcome!<br>
<p>This is my first note
page with a link.</p><br>
<p><a href="Note2.txt">
Click here</a> if you want
to go to my second page.<p>
```

7.14 An example of a note with HTML added to it.

3. **Save this text document with an appropriate name, such as** Note1.txt**. The names you give to your notes are important to remember if you want to link to them.**

4. **Create a new text document with HTML, such as the following:**

```
<TITLE>My Second Note
Page</TITLE>
Welcome!<br>
<p>This is my second note
page with a link.</p><br>
<p><a href="Note1.txt">
Click here</a> if you want
to go to back to my first
page.<p>
```

5. **Save this text document with the name you specified in your first page's link, which in this case is** Note2.txt**.**

6. **Open your iPod with disk mode enabled.**

Linking Notes in Subfolders

To keep your notes organized, particularly if you have dozens, if not hundreds, of notes, you can create subfolders on your iPod. In order to link to note files in these subfolders, modify your link tag to reflect the relative directory, such as `<a href="Folder Name/Note Name">Link Text</a>`. If I had placed the notes inside a subfolder called First Note Tests in the earlier example, a typical link might look like this:

```
<a href="First Note Tests/Note1.txt>Click here</a> to go
to the first note page.
```

7. **Drag-and-drop your note files into the Notes folder.**

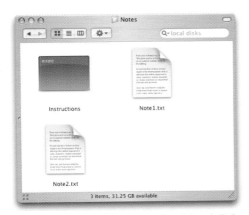

7.15 The Notes folder on an iPod hard disk with text documents.

8. **To read your notes, and test the links, disconnect your iPod (eject the device correctly).**

9. **Choose Extras ⇨ Notes from the iPod's menu.**

10. **Select your first note and click the center Select button to open it.**

11. **Notice your title at the top of the iPod display, and then click the center Select button to activate the link and jump to the next page.** Continue playing with the links, even creating several pages to link between, until you're used to working with HTML and links in note files.

Tip *You can create pages with multiple links. To navigate to a new link, simply scroll down the page using the controls on your iPod, and then click the Select button when the link you want is highlighted.*

Note *You cannot link to notes stored outside the Notes folder on your iPod.*

Linking to songs from within a note file

Because you're creating notes on a portable, flexible music-playing device, it's possible to add links to songs in your iPod's music library. This feature is particularly nice if you have audio lectures or commentary that accompany your notes.

Follow these steps to add a link to a song inside a note on your iPod:

1. **Create a note file as discussed in the previous set of steps.**

2. **Add a link using the following format, which plays a song on your iPod when the link is activated:**

   ```
   <a href="song=
   MyFavoriteSongName">Click
   here</a> to hear my
   favorite song.
   ```

```
● ○ ○                Note3.txt
<TITLE>My Third Note Page</TITLE>
Welcome!<br>
<p>This is my third note page with
links.</p><br>
<p><a href="song=Birthday">Click here</a>
to play my favorite song.</p>
```

7.16 An example of a text file with a link to a song added.

3. **To create another link that accesses a playlist, you can use the format listed here:**

```
<a  href="ipod:music?
playlist=MyFavoritePlay
list">Click here</a> to
hear my favorite playlist.
```

4. **To create another link to access a particular category (album, artist, genre, and so forth) you can use the format listed here:**

```
<a href="ipod:music?
album=MyFavoriteAlbum">
Click here</a> to hear my
favorite album.
```

> **Tip**
>
> *In this example, you can simply substitute "album" for "genre," and so forth.*

5. **To create another link that accesses a particular song on a specific album, you can use the format listed here:**

```
<a href="ipod:music?
album=MyFavoriteAlbum&song
=MyFavorite SongName">
Click here</a> to hear
my favorite song on my
favorite album.
```

6. **When you're done, save the file, and add it to your iPod as you would any other note.** You can navigate using a song link as you would any other link.

> **Note**
>
> *If you click on a song link in a note file and decide while listening to the song that you want to go back, you can simply press the Menu button to return to your notes.*

Checking e-mail on your iPod

As a further extension of the notes and e-book idea, try copying long e-mails into note documents and reading them with your iPod while you're on the road. Better yet, use an application like PodMail for Mac (www.podmail.org) or K-Pod on the PC (www.k-deep.com/k-pod.htm) and sync your IMAP or POP e-mail client with your iPod's Notes folder. These software applications provide a way to make transferring e-mail painless, without requiring endless copying and pasting.

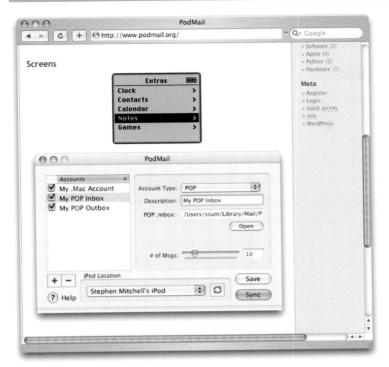

7.17 PodMail for the Mac.

Converting text documents to speech

Depending what computer platform you're working on, or what extra software you have installed, converting text documents to speech can be a simple process. After you've converted a piece of text to spoken work, you might even record it to an audio file and place it on your iPod for hand- and eye-free reading. Perhaps this would be a nice way to create introductions to a song (think Radio Head) or to provide an eerie voiceover effect for a multimedia project.

If you're on a Mac, you can use the built-in text-to-speech function. If you're on a PC, you might try an application like Aldo's Text-to-Wave, 2nd Speech Center, Texthelp systems products, or any of many others that help to convert text to spoken word. Some products read Web pages, PDF documents, and a variety of other text-originated material.

As an example, follow these steps to convert a document to speech (using the Mac, although you can follow a similar workflow on a PC using your application of choice), and then convert it to an audio file that can be copied over to an iPod:

1. **Open the TextEdit application.** Make sure to choose Format ➪ Make Plain Text to remove the Rich Text features that do not work for the HTML document.

2. **Copy and paste some text (such as text from a Web page, an e-mail, a report you have written, or a short story you've found online) into a new TextEdit document.**

3. **Position your cursor at the top of your text document and choose Edit ➪ Speech ➪ Start Speaking.** The built-in voice feature should begin reading the text back to you.

4. **To change the sound of the voice (for example, changing it from a woman to a man or vice versa) open System Preferences, click on the Speech button in** the System Preferences window that appears, and select a new voice from the Default Voice tab in the Speech pane.

5. **Record the spoken voice to an audio file using your Mac's built-in microphone or a separately connected microphone attached to the microphone input, along with a sound application, such as iMovie, Final Cut Pro, SoundTrack, GarageBand, or one of many free sound recorders found online.**

6. **Import your sound file into iTunes as a compressed AAC file (you could also choose to keep it as an AIFF).**

7. **Add your audio to a new playlist and update your iPod with the new file.**

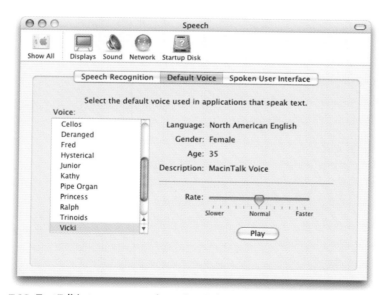

7.18 TextEdit's text-to-speech option is located in the Edit menu, while settings are in the System Preferences Sound menu.

A fun, alternative Web-based tool (cross-platform) for text to speech is under development by AT&T. It is called AT&T Natural Voices Text-to-Speech Engine and can be currently found in a demo stage at `www.naturalvoices.att.com/demos/`. (If the site moves, simply do a search on the project name to find it online, along with a list of alternative services to experiment with.) Although it's limited to 30 words at a time, it provides a relatively natural sounding voice (in a variety of languages with translation) that has some of the usual glitches but is still relatively good. It also produces an audio file for you to manipulate in the format of your choice.

Customizing an iPod

The infinite customizability of the iPod is one of its great appeals. Consider the number of case designs and other add-ons that are available. In this section, I cover a few methods for customizing the look and use of your iPod.

Customizing an iPod with tattoos and graphics

Hewlett-Packard's take on the iPod (with Apple's permission) has spawned the use of *tattoos,* which are simply paper cover printouts that can be wrapped around an iPod. HP Printable Tattoos provide an endless amount of variation for your iPod's look.

You can create your own designs or download the designs of others (including famous artists) to print using special tattoo labels. Look for packs of printable HP

Tattoos at `www.hp.com`, or check with your local computer store, such as Best Buy or Fry's. Tattoos list for about $14.99 on HP's Web site, which includes ten sheets. According to HP, tattoos usually stay affixed for about a month before losing their sticking power. Check out `www.hp.com/music` for more examples and artist downloads (music) including general information about HP's iPod- and iTunes-related products.

Courtesy of HP

7.19 An example of a downloadable HP Tattoo pattern for your iPod.

The truly adventurous users out there are thinking of craft-like project they can do to customize their iPods. One of the more recent examples is taking a pack of gum and turning it into a cover for an iPod shuffle. Of course, painting directly onto your iPod is possible, although it's probably not a good idea if you're afraid of commitment. If you feel the urge to paint up your iPod, try a printable version instead (like the HP Tattoos) or purchase a flat-color case and paint that instead. You might even decide that you like designing cases enough to start up your own company selling original iPod graphics. The possibilities are endless.

Giving your iPod character

A recent (albeit minor) trend seems to be the anthropomorphizing of iPods and their holders. Creating one of the more interesting and accessible examples is Speck Products iGuy (www.speckproducts.com), which is an iPod case that doubles as a toy or desktop companion. With arms and legs, it can stand on its own, or sit in a Dock for recharging. Other users online have created custom stands with figures that hold an iPod or iPod shuffle. This represents just another way that you can extend the enjoyment and appreciation of the iPod.

Courtesy of Speck Products
7.20 The Speck Products iGuy.

Modifying iPod displays

The songs and playlists that you put on your iPod make it unique, as do the cases, sleeves, and tattoos that are added to its outside. Still, wouldn't it be nice if you could have greater control over the way your display looked? Unfortunately, few options are available for altering the color or style of an iPod's screen without some serious hardware modifications or some potentially scary software hacks. Check out user forums online, which may alert you to the latest trends in iPod modifications, including where to find companies that can take a stock iPod, remove its built-in LED and replace it with a different color light (for standard iPods, not including iPod photo). A simple Google search should turn up some results for companies providing those warranty-voiding services.

Installing an iPod in your car

As discussed in Chapter 6, many accessories are available that allow you to play your iPod through an FM radio, including your car's built-in tuner. Some of these devices include the iTrip, a small device that plugs into the top of your iPod, using an FM transmitter to essentially become its own micro radio station, as well as cassette adapters and cigarette-adapter-style transmitters sold by companies like Monster Cable. Monster also makes a device called the iCruze, which installs under the dash of your car (connecting to factory-installed head units) and provides a better, cleaner sounding way for your iPod to interface with your automobile.

Other companies, such as Alpine (KCA-420i) and Dension (iceLink Plus) produce similar devices. You can even go all out and purchase a total A/V experience for your car, complete with iPod support, DVD player, and video screen, such as the Clarion VRX755VD.

Multimedia Techniques

Your iPod can be a useful tool for your next multimedia project, whether it is a simple presentation, a movie, or just for your own enjoyment at home on the couch. In this section, I give you several ideas for using an iPod to help with the creation and viewing of audio, video, and still images.

Creating playlists for multimedia projects

Multimedia projects can benefit from an iPod and iTunes in many ways, particularly if you're using Apple's iLife suite of applications. (iLife software, apart from iTunes, is one of the benefits that comes with working on a Mac.) Even if you're a PC user, you can utilize some of the iTunes features to assist in your next project.

Probably the best use of iTunes for video is its ability to import and sort music and sound effects. The next time you have a video project that requires sound effects or several music cues, consider importing these files into iTunes as AIFF or WAV files, sorting them into playlists, and then exporting the files as needed to your video editing application. Dragging a file from iTunes into a Finder or Explorer window can do the trick after a file is ripped from a CD and placed on your computer. If you're on a Mac, iMovie can do even better, by accessing your iTunes playlists directly from within a built-in browser window.

7.21 iMovie has immediate access to iTunes songs.

Capturing video to an iPod

Although it is certainly not designed for use with video (at least as of this writing), an iPod's function as a FireWire hard drive makes it possible to use for capturing and playing back video when connected to your computer. I don't recommend that you rely on your iPod for this purpose, but it can be a fun test of its functionality and even an interesting benchmark for various video codecs. If you can get video compressed enough to play back smoothly from an iPod, it is a safe bet that it plays back on a standard computer disc drive.

In fact, a company called Blackmagic Design, producers of professional video hardware cards for editing systems like Final Cut Pro, tested the playback of DVCPRO HD content off an iPod successfully. Although it was a flashy statement, it certainly proved the point that the new video format was lean and efficient enough for almost any hard drive to handle.

Using a photo card reader

It used to be that importing photos from a digital camera was a tedious process with bulky attachments. With Apple's introduction of the iPod photo and a special Camera Connector, this process became more streamlined. You can still use a card reader, like the one sold by Belkin, to access cards without the need for your camera, but having more options is nice.

Eventually, it would be great to eliminate the need for a peripheral altogether and simply import from camera directly to iPod photo. For now, the new add-on from Apple is much appreciated and should see a lot of use by digital photographers working in the field, where several gigabytes of hard drive space to back up their work is becoming a necessity (especially as the number of megapixels increases on digital cameras).

Note *The standard iPod, in addition to the iPod photo, is also able to accept photos as files for storage when using a special adapter, such as Belkin's Media Reader.*

Courtesy of Belkin

7.22 Belkin's Media Reader for the iPod is an alternative to Apple's Camera Connector and includes the ability to load photos from a card onto the iPod.

Recording audio with microphones

A variety of audio recording adapters are available for use with an iPod. These include devices by companies such as Belkin and Griffin. Some devices, like Griffin's iTalk, have a built-in microphone, while others, like the Universal Microphone Adapter from Belkin, allow you to attach external microphones.

Unfortunately, the iPod does not currently come with a built-in method for recording audio, although these add-ons do a decent job, particularly as a personal dictation device. The main drawback is that all audio recorded to an iPod (unless running under Linux, as discussed at the end of this chapter) is at an uninspiring 8 kHz, which is fine for most spoken-word recording (lectures, notes to self, and so forth), but far from recording decent quality music, or even producing crystal clear voices.

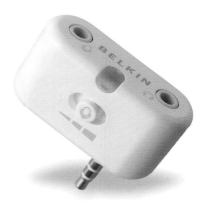

Courtesy of Belkin

7.24 Belkin's Universal Microphone Adapter includes a microphone input for attaching higher quality microphones than might be available on a built-in device.

Creating movies for iPod photo

Although the iPod photo (or any current iPod as of this writing) is not able to play back or view video files, it is possible to cheat a little just for fun. By breaking down a video file into individual frames, you can scrub through the photos using your iPod's Click Wheel controls and simulate a moving image. This is much like playing with a flip-book, proof that old things can become new again. So, if you feel like a digital version of Eadweard Muybridge, follow these steps to create your own "movie" on your iPod photo (with soundtrack). Again, this is simply for fun and should be done with a short

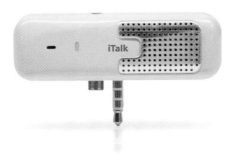

Courtesy of Griffin

7.23 Griffin's iTalk includes a built-in microphone for easy dictation.

clip, because this process requires a lot of images to be effective and can take up a lot of space otherwise.

1. **Locate a video file that you want to use and open in QuickTime Pro, or another video application that allows you to export image sequences.**

2. **Choose File ➪ Export.** The Export Image Sequence Settings dialog box opens.

3. **Select Image Sequence from the Export options and set the file type (in the Options menu) to JPEG.** You can set the Frames Per Second option to match the source video.

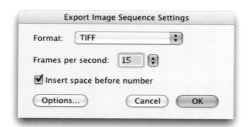

7.25 Exporting a video file as an image sequence.

Note Exporting video as an image sequence can produce up to 1,800 frames per minute for a 30-frames-per-second file.

4. **Make sure your movie file is selected and choose File ➪ Export to export an AIFF (or WAV) file of your movie's audio.**

5. **With your iPod photo attached to your computer, launch iTunes and click the iPod button at the lower-right of the iTunes window.** The Preferences window opens, displaying the iPod pane.

6. **Click on the Photos tab and, in the Synchronize photos from menu, choose the folder containing the image sequence you exported.**

7. **Click OK to close the Preferences window.** The photos are now automatically optimized for playback on your iPod photo, which should take a little while. When finished with the conversion process, your photos are uploaded and ready to be tested. You may also choose to import the audio file you had created, but that isn't necessary.

8. **Eject your iPod and, when the Do Not Disconnect message goes away, disconnect your iPod from your computer.**

9. **On your iPod photo's menu, choose Menu ➪ Photos ➪ Photo Library.**

10. **With your folder of images open on your iPod, use the scroll wheel to quickly rotate forward and backward through the sequence of images.** The smoothness of motion depends on how quickly and steadily you can rotate through the extensive gallery of your video's individual pictures.

Giving PowerPoint and Keynote presentations with iPod photo

iPod photo's ability to create slideshow presentations makes it a natural as a replacement for the traditional PowerPoint presentation. The ability to carry a small device rather than a bulky computer makes this option very appealing – plus, your clients will be impressed by your flashy presentation skills.

In order to get those slides out of PowerPoint (or Keynote for that matter), you need to export them and then add them to iPod photo as you would any other folder of images. You can then arrange these photos into a slideshow.

The following steps demonstrate how to get slides out of PowerPoint for use on an iPod photo. If exporting from Keynote, there is the option to create a QuickTime movie as an interactive slideshow, which can then be exported from QuickTime Pro as an image

sequence. This essentially produces the same results as PowerPoint, and the images may then be uploaded to your iPod photo as outlined in the later steps.

1. **Open a PowerPoint document by clicking on it, or launch PowerPoint and then choose File ⇨ Open to select your presentation.**

2. **When you're finished editing your slides, choose File ⇨ Save As.** The Save As dialog box opens.

3. **Type a name for the presentation.**

4. **Choose JPEG as the format.**

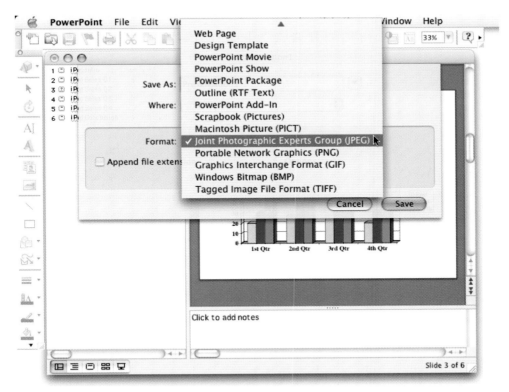

7.26 The JPEG Save option in Microsoft's PowerPoint.

5. **Click the Options button at the bottom of the dialog box.** The Preferences dialog box appears.

6. **Select the Save every slide (series of graphics files) option and click OK.** You want to export every slide not just the current slide.

7. **With your iPod photo attached to your computer, launch iTunes and choose iTunes ➪ Preferences ➪ iPod.** The Preferences window opens.

8. **Click on the Photos pane and, in the Synchronize Photos From menu, choose the folder containing the PowerPoint images you exported.**

9. **Click OK to close the Preferences window.** Your photos are uploaded and ready to become part of a slideshow presentation, as displayed through the video-out capability on your iPod photo.

Podcasting

The iPod's popularity as a personal listening device, combined with the ubiquitous nature of blogging, has spawned a phenomenon known as *podcasting.* The success of podcasting is commonly attributed to Adam Curry (former MTV VJ) who inspired the creation of software to make the process easier.

7.27 Options for exporting slides individually or all at once.

Podcasting is simply a means to quickly and easily transmit Internet radio-style broadcasts that are downloaded onto a user's iPod — think radio blog. The downloading is usually facilitated by software that automates the process with RSS feeds and looks for the latest podcasts online. A podcast can be anything, but it's usually a combination of talk and music. Much like a pirate radio station, podcasts started out generally an underground affair, with extremely limited audiences.

As this book was going to the printer, Apple released iTunes 4.9, with built-in podcast support and access, via the iTunes Music Store, to a vast assortment of podcasts, the majority of which are free. The discussion that follows describes the process for obtaining podcasts that are either not available via the iTunes Music Store or for those of you who cannot (they're using Linux, where iTunes isn't available) or do not want to frequent the iTunes Music Store (some people acknowledge lacking the willpower to see all that great music available and not put a dent in their credit card — out of sight, out of mind). To obtain a podcast via the iTunes Music Store, simply visit the Music Store and click on the Podcasts link in the Choose Store area, try out and select any podcasts of interest, and they will be downloaded to a new Podcasts entry in your Source list.

Anyone with a computer, some cheap software, and a microphone could produce a podcast. However, podcasts are seeing an increase in popularity, thanks to their recent exposure in the media. Even the traditional media has been following the trend, just as they did when blogging become a cultural happening. The democratization of media has taken another step, adding audio to the mix of the global printing press that is the Internet.

To get started with podcasting, pick up a copy of iPodder software (`http://ipodder.sourceforge.net`) and search out some podcasts online. It's available for all computer platforms, including Mac, PC, and GNU/Linux. Also, check out `www.ipodder.org` and `www.dailysourcecode.com` for links to some popular podcasts posted by Adam Curry.

Follow the basic steps outlined here to listen to a podcast:

1. **Download to your computer and install software for receiving podcasts, such as the popular iPodder software from** `http://ipodder.sourceforge.net`.

2. **Launch iPodder.** A window similar to what's shown in figure 7.28 appears.

3. **When you find a podcast online that you want to hear (Podcast Directory tab), click on the link to it.** A file is downloaded immediately to your computer and your iPod, or you can listen to it on your computer.

4. **You can also choose many sites to subscribe to podcast feeds.** Your podcast software (such as iPodder) automatically checks back on a regular basis to automatically pull down new podcasts as they become available.

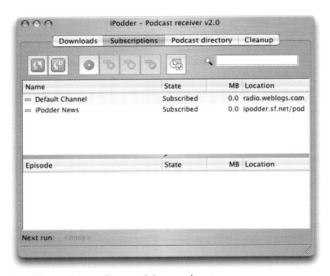

iPodder File Edit View Tools Help

7.28 iPodder software for receiving podcasts.

If you're a budding DJ, why not try putting together you own podcast? Podcasting is already moving into commercial territory, and now is the time to get onboard. It doesn't have to be a daily affair (after all, not many would have the time), but it could be done weekly, or even less frequently, as many amateur podcasts are.

In order to create your own podcasts, the following are some of the elements you should first have in place:

✦ **Computer:** Mac or PC, desktop or laptop.

✦ **Microphone:** Either built-in or attached separately (professional microphones, mixers, and pre-amps require a larger investment but are not necessary).

✦ **Headphones:** For monitoring.

✦ **Audio recording and editing application, such as GarageBand, ProTools, and so on:** Almost any basic recording software works fine, including those that record directly to MP3.

Depending on the way your system is set up, you might need a few more applications to get everything working smoothly. A professional setup would be ideal, but even the most modest audio configuration can work. Regardless of which route you take, you can usually follow the basic workflow in these steps:

1. **Attach a microphone and headphones to your computer.**

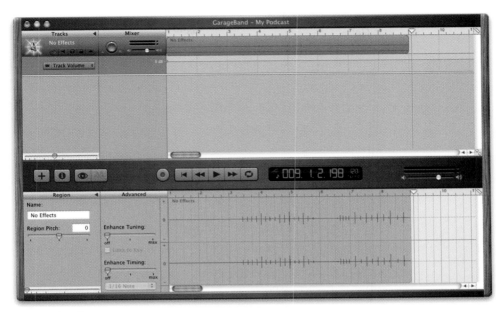

Courtesy of Apple
7.29 GarageBand is a popular audio application that comes with Mac OS X and is able to record audio for use in a podcast.

2. **Install and launch an audio recording application.**

3. **Create a recording of yourself talking about your favorite topic, reading and commenting on news of the day, conducting an interview, whatever.**

4. **Mix the voice recording with some music (not necessary, but a combination of elements — particularly music — is part of what makes a podcast interesting).**

5. **Upload your podcast to your own Web site or a podcast site online.**

Interesting alternatives to the usual methods of producing blogs and podcasts are emerging. One of these is called Audioblogger (www.audioblogger.com), which allows you to post audio to your blog Web site from any phone.

7.30 Audioblogger is a unique service that lets you submit audio blogs from a phone, which other users can access (essentially, a remote podcast).

iPod Hacks

As with any computer device that allows for a degree of programming or hardware and software manipulation, there are many things that you can do to hack or otherwise access unavailable features on your iPod. Although not all the topics discussed in this section are hacks in the traditional sense (after all, scripts are a documented part of the process), they do require some know-how and alterations to make work, just as a programmer or amateur hacker might do.

Introduction to AppleScripts

AppleScript has been a part of the Mac OS for a long time. This feature adds the ability to automate repetitive processes, allowing you to customize the way you work with your Mac and its applications, while saving you time (and potential wrist injury!).

Using AppleScript, you can create a set of routines that would be too complicated or difficult to set up any other way. For example, you could create batch processes that convert files from one format to another, routines that transfer information between databases or link applications together to accomplish related tasks. You can take tasks that you do repeatedly, and create a one-click (or one-drop) operation that does them for you. AppleScripts use a programming language that makes more sense than some other computer languages, because it is based on English rather than obscure computer code.

Using the Script Editor you can create and edit simple scripts in no time. Still, it is a new way of thinking, and putting together the syntax can be a challenge at first, especially for advanced uses. In fact, most of the iTunes and iPod scripts you find are fairly complex. It is beyond the scope of this book to explain the inner workings of AppleScript, although the following sections include examples of scripts in use by iTunes and the iPod.

An example of the simplest AppleScript structure might look like the following (this example shows how to start up iTunes), which shows one way to start and end a script with a `tell` command, while issuing a command to a specific application:

```
tell application "iTunes"
activate
end tell
```

Using AppleScript with iTunes and an iPod

Apple provides some great AppleScript features for use with Mac OS X. You can find these tools by going to `www.apple.com/applescript/itunes`. In addition to the scripts provided by Apple, you can find many others submitted by users on the Web.

The flexibility and (relative) simplicity of AppleScripts makes them fairly abundant among Mac-based iPod users. In fact, you don't have to really know anything about writing an AppleScript to use it. When a collection of scripts is added to iTunes, you can access them through a new Script menu in the bar at the top of the iTunes screen.

Follow these steps to install AppleScripts for iTunes:

1. **Make certain that iTunes is shut down before attempting to install any scripts for the application.**

2. **Download or create AppleScripts that you want to use with iTunes.** You can also use the steps mentioned in the previous section to construct a simple script, or refer to some of the samples in the following section that were provided by Apple.

3. **Open the iTunes folder located in your Home directory's Library folder** (username/Library/iTunes**)**.

Note *There are at least three Library folders on Mac OS X. Make certain that you're looking in the Library folder for the current user, not in the Library folder that is under the Macintosh hard drive. In general, you can usually find your user name in an OS X Finder window's Sidebar (it's the one with the house icon next to it).*

4. **Create a new folder inside your iTunes folder called Scripts.**

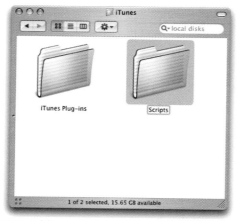

7.31 Adding a Scripts folder to the iTunes folder.

5. **Place all your scripts inside this new folder.**

6. **Launch iTunes and look in the Scripts menu at the top of the screen for all the scripts you've added to the application.**

Sample iTunes scripts

Take a good look at the AppleScripts that follow. Examining the language and structure of scripts is the best way to learn how to create your own. You might start by installing these scripts, seeing how they operate, and then pulling apart the code listed here to figure out what makes them tick. Most of them can be found through Apple's Web site

If you already have scripts on your machine (perhaps you downloaded them from a Web site such as www.dougscripts.com/itunes/), you can use Script Editor to open them, just as you might with a View Source command when visiting a Web site. Simply drag the script file onto the Script Editor application icon (located in your Applications/Apple Script folder) or choose File ➪ Open and select the script you want to view from within the Script Editor application.

The following are a few descriptions of some of the AppleScripts available for download from Apple's Web site. These should give you an idea of what can be done utilizing AppleScripts to automate certain iTunes processes. Although many of these scripts were created back with version 2 of iTunes, they're still usable (AppleScripts are less likely to stop working just because there is a version change in software), although some feature may be obsolete.

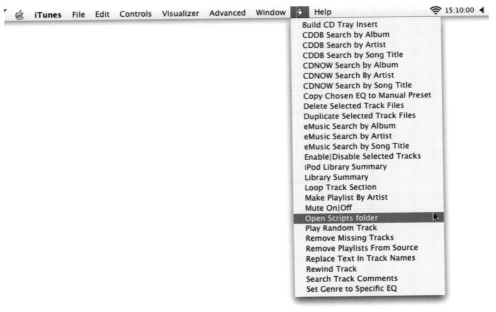

iTunes   File   Edit   Controls   Visualizer   Advanced   Window   ♪   Help   📶 15:10:00 ◀

Build CD Tray Insert
CDDB Search by Album
CDDB Search by Artist
CDDB Search by Song Title
CDNOW Search by Album
CDNOW Search By Artist
CDNOW Search by Song Title
Copy Chosen EQ to Manual Preset
Delete Selected Track Files
Duplicate Selected Track Files
eMusic Search by Album
eMusic Search by Artist
eMusic Search by Song Title
Enable|Disable Selected Tracks
iPod Library Summary
Library Summary
Loop Track Section
Make Playlist By Artist
Mute On|Off
Open Scripts folder
Play Random Track
Remove Missing Tracks
Remove Playlists From Source
Replace Text In Track Names
Rewind Track
Search Track Comments
Set Genre to Specific EQ

7.32 AppleScripts accessed through iTunes.

✦ **Add to iTunes Library.** This script creates a *droplet,* or self-contained application icon that automatically runs a routine for adding files (or folders with several files) dragged onto it into the iTunes library.

✦ **CDDB Search by Album, CDDB Search by Artist, CDDB Search by Song Title.** iTunes has the ability to look up information for a song in the CDDB database manually, although this is still an interesting script to examine, which searches the CDDB database using the info of the selected track.

✦ **Duplicate Selected Track Files.** Use this script to easily duplicate any tracks you select to a new destination on your computer (good for creating copies of files you might want to use for video editing, for example, although there are other scripts out there specifically for this purpose).

✦ **Enable|Disable Selected Tracks.** You can quickly enable or disable selected tracks with this script (the blue checkmark to the left of a song).

✦ **iPod Library Summary.** This script creates a summary list of all the tracks on your iPod.

✦ **Library Summary.** This script quickly creates a summary list of all the tracks in your iTunes Library.

✦ **Loop Track Section.** This script sets start and end points for a loop using the current playback position for a selected track. To operate, simply move the song's playhead indicator to where you want the loop to begin and then run the script and set the start point. To set the end point for the loop, move the playhead to where you want the loop to end and then run the script again and set the end point. You may then run the script one last time to play the section you designated to loop. Open the script again to stop the loop's playback.

✦ **Make Playlist by Artist.** Creates a playlist containing all the tracks of a chosen artist.

✦ **Open Scripts Folder.** In case you don't want to go searching for it, this script opens the Scripts folder in your iTunes folder (if you want to add, delete, or inspect scripts).

✦ **Play Random Track.** Plays a randomly selected track. Although Shuffle and Party Shuffle modes do this now, it could be a good script to analyze for learning how to use AppleScripts.

✦ **Remove Missing Tracks.** Removes tracks associated with files that are missing.

✦ **Remove Playlists from Source.** Deletes playlists from any source that is selected.

✦ **Replace Text in Track Names.** This script can be used to find or change text that is in a song's name.

✦ **Rewind Track.** Another beginner script (useful for analysis) that moves the playhead back to the start of a track.

✦ **Search Track Comments.** Searches the comment field of tracks and creates a playlist that contains tracks with matching information (for instance, you could flag a song with a special word in the comment's field).

✦ **Set Genre to Specific EQ.** This script sets the EQ of all tracks in a selected genre to a specific preset.

Unfortunately, most of these scripts are too long to fit in the pages of this book. As an example, and one of the shorter scripts mentioned, figure 7.33 includes a partial example of a Loop Track Section script. Download the scripts from Apple's site and inspect them more closely.

Sample iPod scripts

iTunes is not the only one that can benefit from the use of AppleScripts. In fact, scripts for the iPod are some of the most useful, particularly when working with notes. Notes can become unruly if you have too many of them or if you want to break up larger blocks of text to fit within the 4KB-per-note text limit.

Many of the AppleScripts for the iPod require the use of a Script Menu utility, which runs the script with or without a host application (visit www.apple.com/applescript/scriptmenu/ for more information). In addition to Script Menu, if your ScriptEditor application is running, you can also double-click on one of these scripts and then click the Run button to initiate the operation.

```
● ● ●                          🔧 Loop Track Section                                    ⬭
┌──────────────────────────────────────────────────────────────────────────────────────┐
│  ◯        ⬤        ▶        ⟨                                                          │
│ Record   Stop     Run     Compile                                                      │
├──────────────────────────────────────────────────────────────────────────────────────┤
│ property required_version : "2.0.3"                                                    │
│                                                                                        │
│ property start_time : 0                                                                │
│ property end_time : 0                                                                  │
│ property track_length : 0                                                              │
│                                                                                        │
│ tell application "iTunes"                                                              │
│      activate                                                                          │
│      try                                                                               │
│           -- VERSION CHECK                                                             │
│           set this_version to the version as string                                   │
│           if this_version is not greater than or equal to the required_version then    │
│                beep                                                                     │
│                display dialog "This script requires iTunes version: " & required_version & ¬ │
│                     return & return & ¬                                                │
│                     "Current version of iTunes: " & this_version buttons {"Update", "Cancel"} default button 2 with icon 2 │
│                if the button returned of the result is "Update" then                   │
│                     my access_website("http://www.apple.com/itunes/download/")         │
│                     return "incorrect version"                                         │
│                end if                                                                   │
│           end if                                                                        │
│           -- stop                                                                       │
│           try                                                                           │
│                set the total_seconds to the duration of the current track              │
│                set the total_seconds to the total_seconds as integer                   │
│           on error                                                                      │
│                error "There is no current track."                                      │
│           end try                                                                       │
│                                                                                        │
│           display dialog "Play the track or set the loop start and end points?" buttons {"Cancel", "Play", "Set"} │
│           if the button returned of the result is "Set" then                           │
│                set the current_time to the player position                             │
│                display dialog "Set the current time as the start or end of the loop?" & ¬ │
│                     return & return & ¬                                                 │
│                     "Current time (in seconds): " & (current_time as string) & return & ¬ │
│                     "Loop start: " & (start_time as string) & return & ¬               │
│                     "Loop end: " & (end_time as string) buttons {"Cancel", "Start", "End"} │
├──────────────────────────────────────────────────────────────────────────────────────┤
│                          [ Description ] [ Result ] [ Event Log ]                       │
└──────────────────────────────────────────────────────────────────────────────────────┘
```

7.33 A portion of the Loop Track Section script.

The following represent some AppleScripts you can download from Apple's Web site or create yourself to help manage your iPod, iPod photo, or iPod mini better (check out www.apple.com/applescript/ipod/).

✦ **Eject iPod.** A simple script that allows you to quickly eject an iPod that is currently mounted to your computer.

✦ **Clear All Notes.** Just like it says, this script deletes all the notes in the Notes folder on your iPod, including an option to remove sub-folders if they exist.

✦ **Clipboard to Note.** By simply copying text from any document using the standard copy command (Edit ➪ Copy or ⌘+C) and then running this script, you can automatically create a new note that is placed on your iPod containing the text. Longer documents that exceed the 4KB limit are instantly divided and placed into multiple note files.

✦ **List Notes.** A basic script that displays any notes you have currently installed on your iPod, providing a quick way to access and edit files.

✦ **Note from Web Pages.** A useful script that can extract articles from the Web and place them into note files for use on an iPod. This script works solely with Safari (although I suppose you could modify it to work with another browser), and includes a Printer Friendly script that improves your notes by removing most of the ads or other Web-only items that can create a lot of cluttered code in your note files.

Because most of these scripts are too long to fit in the pages of this book, a portion of one of the shorter scripts mentioned is listed in figure 7.34 (a Clipboard to Note script). Once again, it is suggested that you download the scripts from Apple's site and inspect them more closely.

Installing Linux on an iPod

There is a whole universe of possibilities for the iPod as you head into the future. One of the most interesting worlds that we can explore today is the one brought about by the merger of the iPod and Linux. The popularity of Linux, an open-source operating system that is constantly improved upon by its users, has resulted in a wide range of free products that anyone can use.

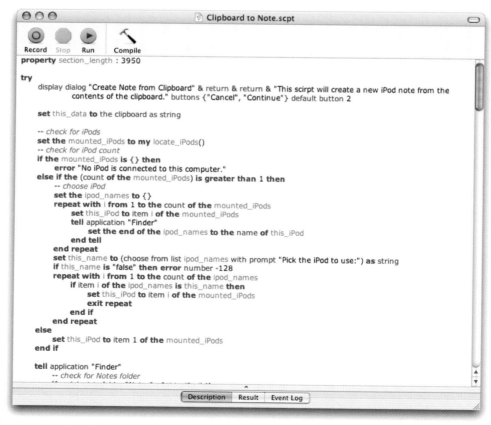

7.34 A portion of the Clipboard to Note script.

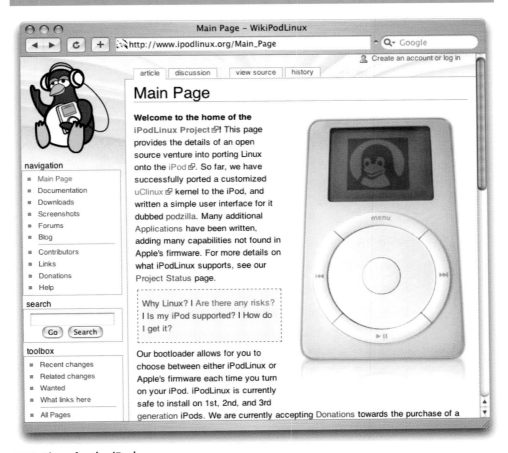

7.35 Linux for the iPod.

You can see one of these free products by visiting the iPodLinux Project Web site (www.ipodlinux.org). A version of Linux for the iPod along with a simple interface called podzilla can be downloaded. As of this writing, only third-generation iPods and earlier are working consistently with this software, although a version for 4G iPods is in development. After you've installed Linux on your iPod, you can access all sorts of applications, which open up capabilities that were not possible before on an iPod. For example, audio can be recorded at much higher quality (96 kHz versus 8 kHz) and additional games can be played.

The following steps illustrate the basic process for installing a version of Linux on your iPod and booting up under the new OS.

Note *Playing songs under Linux on an iPod is prone to playback problems. I recommend that you reboot into the original iPod operating system when you want to listen to music.*

1. **Make certain your iPod is plugged into your computer and disk mode is enabled.**

2. **Run the Linux installer.**

3. **When the installer is finished, eject the iPod from your computer.**

4. **Reboot your iPod by holding down the Menu and Play buttons until the Apple logo appears.**

5. **When you see the Apple logo, press and hold down the Back button.** You should now see the Linux mascot appear on the iPod's screen (Linux's mascot is a Penguin called Tux) and the new system interface (podzilla) should appear momentarily. Within this new interface, additional options are available.

6. **To go back to the iPod operating system at any time while in Linux, hold down the Menu and Play buttons to reset the iPod.** You can switch back and forth between the two operating systems whenever you want.

iPod Maintenance and Troubleshooting

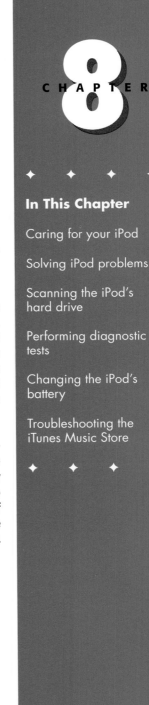

A s with any electronic or computer device, there are always times when problems arise that need fixing. Despite its simple design and legendary ease of use, the iPod is no exception. In fact, as it becomes more popular and the device is produced on a mass scale, additional problems are bound to surface. Still, in terms of microcomputers, the iPod is amazingly reliable and when problems arise, solving them with only a little guidance is often possible.

In this chapter, I cover some of the methods for solving common iPod problems and glitches, and introduce some of the concepts necessary to investigate solutions to those relatively rare malfunctions that may occur. Ideally, you'll never need to use this chapter, although familiarizing yourself with some of the topics discussed here is still a good idea, whether you're fixing your own iPod or giving advice to friends and family. Prepare for the worst and hope for the best.

Caring for Your iPod

An iPod, although a reasonably rugged and well-built device, is still a computer, and thus a sensitive electronic instrument that needs a certain degree of care to keep it running smoothly. The first thing that you can do to ensure a long life for your iPod is to protect it with a case and store it properly, preferably in a place where it won't get dropped easily, have pressure applied to it, or be subjected to extreme hot and cold temperatures. Because it has a hard drive or, in the case of an iPod shuffle, uses flash memory, keeping your iPod away from strong magnetic fields, such as the top of a speaker enclosure, is also important.

In addition to these common-sense precautions, keeping your iPod clean and free from dirt is also important. Even if you're using a case, an iPod is susceptible to dust, smudges, and scratches. Use a soft cloth, without harsh surface cleaners, to periodically wipe off your iPod's display, along with the back of its case (the shiny metal housing picks up fingerprints and oil very easily).

iPod Updater

Apple's iPod Updater software is used to add new features or fixes to your iPod software. You can also use it to restore the factory settings on your iPod; it erases all

current songs and data while performing a clean install on the hard drive. This is generally done as a last resort when all other options are exhausted. Although your data will be erased when using the restore function, the data can be added back by re-synching with iTunes after the update is complete. Check the Apple site periodically for new software, or use the Software Update feature to check for new versions (if you are working on a Mac).

8.1 iPod Updater software supports the various iPod models.

8.2 Run iPod Updater software to restore an iPod to its factory settings or to remain current with the latest firmware fixes.

Solving iPod Problems

The following sections are a collection of some commonly encountered iPod problems and suggested solutions. Although not every problem has an easy solution, most can be worked through by referring to these steps or by looking on Apple's support site for more documentation. Also, many Web sites have popped up with user forums with friendly iPod owners that may help answer your questions. Occasionally, a serious problem occurs that can only be fixed by sending your iPod in for repairs. Before taking that step, refer to some of the topics listed here, or conduct some more research online. In general, before doing anything else, make sure that your iPod has been updated with the latest software and firmware.

Note *For the most stubborn problems, you should reset your iPod (as described earlier in this chapter) and then restore it using iPod Updater.*

Songs skip

If you're using any of the iPod models other than iPod shuffle, your device is susceptible to skipping. Although the built-in skip protection goes a long way to prevent this type of mishap, it can still happen. The following sections suggest a few ways you can prevent your music from skipping.

Use compressed song formats

iPods are designed for playing back compressed audio files. In particular, an iPod's skip protection, which is limited to about 32MB in size, was designed with smaller files in mind. It is also the small size of files, such as those downloaded from the iTunes Music Store, that make it possible to fit 10,000 or more songs on a device. By including uncompressed files on your iPod (such as AIFF or WAV files), especially songs that are longer in length, the hard drive has to do more work, because it needs to access information more often and cannot rely on its cache to hold the files. The more a hard drive spins, the greater its chance of being shaken or subjected to shocks that can make it skip.

Make sure that the majority of songs you play on your iPod are compressed to a format like AAC or MP3 for greatest efficiency of space, as well as the best hard drive and skip-protection performance. Because they're smaller than the cache, compressed files require less battery power, as the hard drive doesn't have to spin as much (cache uses much less power). Apple recommends that the average size of files be kept under 9MB. That doesn't mean you can't use larger files; it just means that these file sizes provide the best performance overall. You may even choose to break up longer songs into smaller files to improve results.

Check your music files for damage

Sometimes, the problem isn't with your iPod but with the files you place on it. Before assuming that your iPod is responsible for performance issues, make sure that your music is not the real culprit. If skipping occurs on one or more files, try deleting those files, re-importing them from a CD (of course, this doesn't work if your music was purchased online), and re-uploading them to your iPod.

Avoid shaking the iPod

iPods rely on skip protection to prevent songs from skipping when the device is subjected to hard impacts, as when you're jogging. Usually, the memory cache does a great job by holding song information in memory until it needs to check the hard drive for more. A standard iPod and iPod mini have 25 minutes of built-in skip protection (the iPod photo has 17 minutes), which means that several songs can be copied into a memory cache (approximately

32MB capacity) at one time. In some situations, the iPod's hard drive might skip if it's shaken while trying to access more songs to refill its cache (after it has finished playing the songs you selected, or you skip a selection). Try to be gentle with your iPod when possible, or purchase an iPod shuffle for use during sports and other physical activity. The iPod shuffle's use of flash memory and lack of a hard drive make it impervious to skips caused by impacts because there is no moving mechanism that can skip.

Reset the iPod

An iPod that skips when there is no obvious reason may need to be reset. In general, resetting is a good way to overcome problems, particularly if you're unsure of the exact cause. Holding down the Menu and Select buttons for several seconds resets most iPod models. The pre-4G models require holding down the Menu and Play/Pause buttons for several seconds.

Restore the iPod

Restoring is done as a last resort, if all other options fail and your iPod continues to malfunction. When you restore an iPod, all data is lost and your device is wiped clean. The restoration process cannot be undone. Make sure you have a backup of all your files before following this course of action.

iPod freezes

Sometimes, an iPod freezes while connecting, disconnecting, or simply just sitting there. Before you try anything else, make sure the iPod is unpaused and the Hold switch is not in the locked position. Also, make certain that you've correctly ejected the iPod from your computer (this means waiting for the "Do not disconnect." warning to go away before ejecting). After you've determined that your iPod is not functioning correctly, you can try resetting it, which usually solves the freezing problem. The methods for resetting your iPod vary slightly according to the model that you own.

Note *Resetting your iPod does not affect music and data files, although some customized settings may be lost.*

To reset an iPod (4G with Click Wheel), iPod photo, or iPod mini, follow these steps:

1. **Disconnect the iPod from your computer if it is currently connected.**

2. **Toggle the Hold switch on the top of your iPod on and off.**

3. **Press and hold the Menu and Select buttons at the same time, until the Apple logo appears.** If a logo does not appear in about ten seconds, you may need to repeat this step, or try resetting using one of the other sets of iPod instructions.

Tip *If you're having trouble getting these instructions to work, try connecting your iPod to a power source, such as a separate power adapter, while performing these steps.*

To reset an iPod (1G with Scroll Wheel, 2G and 3G with Touch Wheel), follow these steps:

1. **Disconnect the iPod from your computer if it is currently connected.**

2. **Toggle the Hold switch on the top of your iPod on and off.**

3. **Press and hold the Play/Pause and Menu buttons at the same time, until the Apple logo appears.** If a logo does not appear in about ten seconds, you may need to repeat this step, or try resetting using one of the other sets of iPod instructions.

To reset an iPod shuffle, follow these steps:

1. **Disconnect the iPod shuffle from your computer if it is currently connected.**

2. **Slide the switch on the back of the iPod shuffle to off, which is the top position (the green stripe should not be visible).**

3. **After waiting several seconds, slide the switch to one of the playback positions, such as Play in Order or Shuffle.** If this doesn't cure the problem, you should take your iPod to an Apple dealer.

iTunes freezes

If iTunes freezes while ejecting an iPod, it may be because the iPod was not disconnected properly. Make sure you wait for the "Do not disconnect." warning to go away before shutting down iTunes or removing your iPod (click the Eject button for your iPod to remove it, or drag its disc icon to the trash, if working on a Mac). If iTunes freezes, you may simply need to force-quit the software and relaunch the application. Try waiting for iTunes to launch before reconnecting your iPod to the computer.

8.3 Wait for the "Do not disconnect." warning to disappear before removing your iPod or shutting down iTunes.

iPod does not connect with computer

If you're experiencing connection problems between your iPod and computer, first make sure that your computer is recognizing the FireWire or USB port you're plugging your iPod into. Start by unplugging the iPod and plugging it back in. If that doesn't work, check system information about your computer, to confirm that its ports are working properly.

On a Mac, this information is listed in the System Profiler, which is accessed through the Apple menu. Select About this Mac, and then click the More Info button.

There is a similar method on PCs that involves going to the Properties option for My Computer or clicking System in the Control Panel. If the FireWire or USB port is not showing an attached device, there could be a larger problem, such as bad ports or cables. Try plugging it into an alternate FireWire or USB port or switching cables to test these premises.

In general, when an iPod refuses to make a connection with your computer, it displays an Apple logo, like the one you see at the startup screen. You can try disconnecting your iPod, forcing it into disk mode by holding down the Menu and Play buttons to restart it, and then holding down the Next and Previous buttons when the screen returns to the Apple logo. After confirming that disk mode is displayed, you can plug it into your computer. If nothing happens (the iPod should appear on the desktop), you might consider connecting it with a different computer as a test, resetting it as described in an earlier section, or (after all else fails) restoring your iPod to its factory settings. Hopefully, it's a problem that can be resolved without sending your iPod into Apple for servicing.

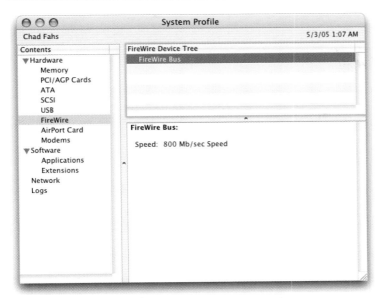

8.4 Apple's System Profiler.

iPod does not charge

Usually when your iPod refuses to charge, it's because it's attached to a sleeping computer. To initiate charging, wake up your computer by opening its lid (on a laptop) or activating a key on your keyboard. If this is not the problem, your USB or FireWire cable may be faulty and need replacing. Additionally, placing an iPod in a chain with other FireWire devices might be resulting in a power drain that is not sufficient to provide power to the iPod.

Note *When using FireWire on a Windows computer, you occasionally encounter situations where the FireWire port does not provide power – these are typically characterized by requiring a 4-pin FireWire connector or being situated on a PC card. If you encounter such a situation, you should charge your iPod using the AC adapter/recharger.*

Music does not play after formatting or partitioning as a hard drive

As a word of caution, do not attempt to reformat your iPod using Disk Utility (in Mac OS X) or another utility, including Windows Explorer on the PC, unless it's absolutely necessary. Reformatting, and repartitioning, results in the loss of access to your music files. The reason is that an iPod can only be used as true music player (the way you ordinarily listen to it while on the move) if it is formatted in a specific way. For Macs, this means that the iPod must be in the Mac OS Extended (HFS Plus) format, while PCs must use FAT32. Whatever you do, do not reformat an iPod using Mac OS Standard (HFS) or UNIX File System (UFS). The only exception here is the iPod shuffle, which should always use FAT32.

If your iPod's hard drive was accidentally reformatted using a different type of disk volume, you can always restore it back to its factory settings by installing the latest iPod Updater application on your computer and following the steps to restore factory defaults. The biggest drawback to restoring an iPod is that you'll lose all data, including songs, photos, and all other files. Hopefully, you'll have all these files backed up on your computer (assuming you've been managing and syncing with iTunes all along). Restoring defaults is always a last step in getting your iPod to work properly.

Audio static occurs

Audio problems — whether static, pops, or other forms of interference — can be extremely distracting, even ruining the music listening experience. No one should have to put up with static on an iPod. Unfortunately, if you're hearing consistent noise that is not related to the music files or your headphones (to make certain, test your headphones and your song files on another computer or audio device), it may be your iPod. There have been a few reports in the past of faulty devices, such as problems that result in crackling sounds. Although this is not the experience of most users, these sorts of problems do occur from time to time with any electronic device. However, it is more likely that the static is a combination of factors related to song files, iPod firmware, and accessories that you may have attached to the device (such as an iTrip, camera attachment, and so on). Disconnect any accessories you may have connected to the iPod and restart the device. If the problem persists, reset your iPod, and make sure to install the latest drivers and firmware, which can be downloaded from the Apple site.

Note *You may hear a whirring sound through your headphones when waiting for a song to load on your iPod, iPod photo, or iPod mini. This is the sound of the iPod's hard drive spinning up to access the data you've requested. It is a normal sound and not a malfunction. If you want to avoid this sound as much as possible, use playlists rather than skipping songs with the Next and Previous buttons. Songs that are read from the cache do not create this noise.*

Scanning the iPod's Hard Drive

When things go wrong with your iPod's hard drive, it has a built-in method called Disk Scan for trying to find and deal with the problem. Disk Scan launches automatically when it is needed, usually when you turn on your iPod. You'll know when your iPod enters Disk Scan mode, because an icon that looks like a magnifying glass on top of a round disc appears on your iPod's screen.

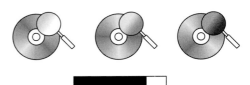

8.5 The Disk Scan icons indicate that your iPod's hard drive is being searched for problems.

The entire Disk Scan process can take quite a while, up to 20 minutes, so be patient and let the iPod do its job. A series of diagnostic tools check your disk for any damage that may have occurred and make an effort to repair it. When a problem is found, or Disk Scan reaches the end of its process, another icon alerts you to the specific nature of the problem. Ideally, no issues are found and your iPod is given a clean bill of health. If the problem is irreparable, you may need to ship your iPod into Apple for repairs. Before you do that, try resetting the device and restoring the factory defaults on the device using the iPod Software Updater.

Note   *The iPod Service Web site is at* `http://depot.info.apple.com/ipod.`

Tip   *You can cancel the Disk Scan process while it's in progress by holding down the center Select button for a few seconds. The iPod should resume Disk Scan when it starts up the next time.*

The following figures show the five possible screens that may appear after Disk Scan has run its diagnostics.

8.6 No issues found.

8.7 Disk Scan failed and will repeat the next time you turn on your iPod.

8.8 Problems with hard drive were found, and some or all were repaired.

8.9 Disk Scan was canceled by user.

8.10 A sad iPod icon indicates that data cannot be recovered and your iPod requires professional repairs.

Performing Diagnostic Tests

For tech-savvy users who are willing to do some investigating, several useful diagnostic tools and tests are built into the iPod. To access the iPod's diagnostics, follow these steps:

1. **Make sure the iPod is plugged into a power source, such as an AC adapter, or a FireWire port on a computer.**

2. **Reset the iPod by holding down the Menu and Select buttons for about ten seconds.** You hold down Menu and Play/Pause on some earlier models.

3. **When the Apple logo appears, press and hold down the Previous and Select buttons on 4G models and the mini.** You hold down Previous, Next, and center Select buttons on earlier models. A list of tests will appear on the screen.

4. **Navigate through the various test pages and options, using the Next and Previous buttons.** Pressing Select activates a test, while pressing the Play button returns to the original diagnostic screen.

5. **When you're finished checking out the various tests, press and hold the Menu and Select buttons for several seconds to reset the iPod and exit the diagnostic mode.**

Changing the iPod's Battery

As your iPod grows older, its lithium-ion battery's ability to hold a charge inevitably fades. Unfortunately, changing the iPod's battery is not a simple or inexpensive process that can easily be performed from home. It takes some technical know-how and an adventurous spirit to crack that case for the first time.

If you're itching to see what's inside your iPod's case (which is not recommended, particularly for the average user), you'll need a flathead screwdriver and some pliers. Damage to the case is a real possibility, so be warned.

 Caution *By opening the iPod and attempting to change the battery, you likely void your Apple warranty, even if you have an AppleCare plan.*

So what are you to do if your battery dies or is in need of replacing? The first, and safest option is to send it back to Apple for their official battery-replacement service. This service currently costs $99 and is well worth it, considering the hassle (and potential damage) of doing it yourself. An alternative option would be to ship it to another company that is willing to do the replacement for a lower price. There are many companies out there that will do this for you, although it will probably still cost around $79 for the battery and service.

If you're concerned about the performance and longevity of your battery, you can do a few things to keep it running smoothly before it needs replacing:

✦ **Keep it cool.** Operate your iPod within factory-recommended temperatures (32°F to 95°F or 0°C to 35°C). When not in use, store the iPod within an acceptable range of temperatures (−4°F to 113°F or −20°C to 45°C). Whatever you do, don't leave your iPod in the car on a hot day, where temperatures can reach in excess of 150°F (65°C). This also applies to leaving the iPod in direct sunlight for extended periods of time. Apple also recommends not charging the iPod in its case or cover, because it can trap heat while drawing power to charge the battery, although this is less of a concern than the other situations mentioned.

✦ **Put the iPod to sleep.** When the iPod is not in use, make sure you put it into Sleep mode to conserve battery power. You can simply press and hold the Play button until it goes to sleep.

✦ **Charge frequently.** Make sure that you charge the battery often, even if you aren't using the iPod for extended periods of time. It's generally recommended that you charge the battery every 14 to 18 days, even if it isn't in use. When the iPod is turned off, it's really in a sleeping mode that still draws power. It's harder on the battery if it's left to drain and not kept in a charged state than if you keep it charged. It also makes it less convenient when you *do* want to use your iPod!

Troubleshooting the iTunes Music Store

As with any other application or Web site, the iTunes Music Store is not immune to problems. Occasionally, you might encounter a few hiccups while using the service. On the rare occasion that your computer or Internet connection crashes while buying and downloading music, once you log back in to iTunes, you can choose Advanced ⇨ Check for Purchased Music. Any songs that have been purchased but not downloaded should automatically be downloaded to your computer at that time.

8.11 Assistance with the iTunes Music Store can be found in the iTunes Help menu.

You can contact the customer service department of the iTunes Music Store at any time by choosing Music Store Customer Service from the iTunes Help menu.

 Tip

Make sure you keep a backup of all your files on a separate drive, or burn them to disc for safekeeping. Because, unfortunately, if your computer's hard drive crashes and your music files are lost, you cannot download them again. Although Apple keeps track of your purchase history, it doesn't allow you to download music a second time.

Appendixes

iPod and iTunes Resources

A wide variety of iPod resources are out there for just about any iPod- or iTunes-related topic you can think of. This appendix lists a few of the popular sites that you might encounter, although it is by no means complete. New Web sites and companies that produce products for iPods are popping up every day, so keep a look out for new and better sources of information.

General iPod and iTunes News, Information, and Support

The following items represent a cross section of some iPod-related sites. Many of these sites also include user forums and support information for troubleshooting problems you may encounter.

www.portablepop.com

The Web site of this book's author, which contains links and information to iPod and iTunes resources, as well as information on other portable devices, such as Sony's PSP, and new cellular technology with a focus on audio, video, and multimedia features.

www.apple.com/itunes

The official Apple home page for iPod and iTunes products.

www.apple.com/ipod

The official Apple home page for iPod products.

www.apple.com/support/ipod

Apple's support site for iPod-, iPod photo-, and iPod mini-related questions.

www.apple.com/support/ipodshuffle

Apple's support site for iPod shuffle-related questions.

www.apple.com/support/itunes

Apple's support site for iTunes Mac-related questions.

www.apple.com/support/itunes/windows

Apple's support site for iTunes Windows-related questions.

http://en.wikipedia.org/wiki/ipod

An amazing site, maintained by users, that contains information and links about any iPod-related topic imaginable. Make sure to check this one out.

www.howstuffworks.com

A nicely designed site that provides some of the best explanations around. A great tool for anyone looking to understand the inner workings of a device or technical subject. Look up information for iPod, podcasting, MP3, and other related topics. Highly addictive.

www.ipodlounge.com

iPod Lounge is one of the best sources for iPod news and reviews on the Web. It also produces a substantial (and free) buyer's guide that you can download, featuring detailed descriptions and filled with colorful photographs. Make sure to bookmark this site.

www.everythingipod.com

If you're looking for a particular iPod accessory, you'll probably find it here.

www.ipoding.com

Another site for general iPod news and support information.

www.ipodhacks.com

Although a bit odd to navigate (like other blog style sites), this is a good source for finding user-submitted iPod hacks and other modification information.

www.ipodstudio.com

Yet another general news and information site for iPod-related products.

www.ipodstyles.com

Browse a selection of iPod cases and sleeve designs.

iPod Manufacturer Web Sites

The following is a list of a few companies that produce iPod-related products, including hardware and software. This list is by no means exhaustive, although many of these companies sell items that are discussed in the pages of this book.

Apple

www.apple.com/store

The obvious choice for many of your iPod needs! Apple also has many stores located in malls and shopping centers around the world where you can find plenty of iPod products in stock.

Griffin

www.griffintechnology.com

Griffin produces a wide variety of iPod accessories.

Belkin

www.belkin.com

Like Griffin, Belkin produces a wide range of useful devices for your iPod.

DLO

www.dlodirect.com

Producers of iPod cases, speakers, and other accessories.

Logitech

www.logitech.com

Creators of computer peripherals and some iPod-related accessories, including speakers.

Monster Cable

www.monstercable.com

In addition to selling high-end audio and video cables, Monster sells a selection of iPod peripherals, including car adapters.

JBL

www.jbl.com

A producer of speakers and speaker systems for iPods. You can find this brand for purchase through Web sites like the Apple Store, Amazon.com, or some of the general information sites listed at the beginning of this appendix.

Bose

www.bose.com

A producer of speakers and speaker systems for iPods. You can find this brand for purchase through Web sites like the Apple Store, Amazon.com, or some of the general information sites listed at the beginning of this appendix.

Altec Lansing

www.alteclansing.com

A producer of speakers and speaker systems for iPods. You can find this brand for purchase through Web sites like the Apple Store, Amazon.com, or some of the general information sites listed at the beginning of this appendix.

Tivoli Audio

www.tivoliaudio.com

A producer of speakers and speaker systems for iPods. You can find this brand for purchase through Web sites like the Apple Store, Amazon.com, or some of the general information sites listed at the beginning of this appendix.

Etymotic Research, Inc.

www.etymotic.com

Creators of high-quality earphones for discerning listeners.

iPodder

http://ipodder.sourceforge.net

Cross-platform podcasting software (Mac, PC, GNU/Linux), originally conceived of by the "father" of podcasting, Adam Curry.

iPodderX

http://ipodderx.com

Podcasting software for the Mac.

Keyboard Shortcuts

iTunes provides keyboard and mouse-click shortcuts for most of its menu commands and buttons. The tables in this appendix collect and summarize these shortcuts for you.

Table B.1
Playback Control Shortcuts

Description	Mac	PC
Play Selected Song	Return	Enter
Play Next Album in List	Option+Right Arrow	Shift+Ctrl+Alt+Right Arrow
Play Previous Album in List	Option+Left Arrow	Shift+Ctrl+Alt+Left Arrow
Fast-Forward to Next Song in List	⌘+Right Arrow	Right Arrow
Rewind to Previous Song in List	⌘+Left Arrow	Left Arrow
Stop or Start Playing Song	Spacebar	Spacebar
Play Next Song in List (While Another Song Is Playing)	⌘+Right Arrow	Right Arrow
Play Previous Song in List (While Another Song Is Playing)	⌘+Left Arrow	Left Arrow
Go to Next Chapter of Audible Spoken-Word File (If Available)	⌘+Shift+Right Arrow	Ctrl+Shift+Right Arrow
Go to Previous Chapter of Audible Spoken-Word File (If Available)	⌘+Shift+Right Arrow	Ctrl+Shift+Right Arrow
Increase Volume	⌘+Up Arrow	Ctrl+Up Arrow
Decrease Volume	⌘+Down Arrow	Ctrl+Down Arrow
Mute Sound	Option+⌘+Down Arrow	Ctrl+Shift+Down Arrow
Eject CD	⌘+E	Ctrl+E

Table B.2
File and Playlist Shortcuts

Description	Mac	PC
Create New Playlist	⌘+N	Ctrl+N
Create Playlist from Selected Songs	Shift+⌘+N	Ctrl+Shift+N
Create New Smart Playlist	Option+Click the Add (+) Button or Option+⌘+N	Shift+Click the Add (+) Button or Ctrl+Alt+N
Reshuffle Current Playlist	Option+Click the Shuffle Button	Shift+Click the Shuffle Button
Delete Selected Playlist from Source List	⌘+Delete	Ctrl+Delete

Description	Mac	PC
Delete Selected Playlist and Its Songs from Library	Option+Delete	Shift+Delete
Delete Selected Songs from Library and All Playlists	Option+Delete	Shift+Delete
Add File to Library	⌘+O	Ctrl+O
Close iTunes Window	⌘+W	Ctrl+W
Import a Song, Playlist, or Library File	Shift+⌘+O	Ctrl+Shift+O
Check or Uncheck All Songs in List	⌘+Click Checkbox for Song	Ctrl+Click Checkbox for Song
Change Song Info Columns	Control+Click Column Heading	Right-Click Column Heading
Get Info for Selected Song or Album	⌘+I	Ctrl+I
Get Info for Next Song in List (While in Get Info Window)	⌘+N	Ctrl+N
Get Info for Previous Song in List (While in Get Info Window)	⌘+P	Ctrl+P
Go to Next Pane in Get Info or Preferences Window	⌘+Right Bracket ( ])	Ctrl+Right Bracket ( ])
Go to Previous Pane in Get Info or Preferences Window	⌘+Left Bracket ([ )	Ctrl+Left Bracket ([ )
Show Location of Song File	⌘+R	Ctrl+R
Show Currently Playing Song in List	⌘+L	Ctrl+L

Table B.3
Window and View Shortcuts

Description	Mac	PC
Close iTunes Window	⌘+W	Ctrl+W
Hide iTunes Window	⌘+H	Ctrl+H
Hide All Other Applications	Option+⌘+H	N/A
Quit iTunes	⌘+Q	Ctrl+Q
Shrink iTunes Window (Only Playback Controls or Mini Player Window)	Click Zoom Control in Upper-Left Corner of iTunes Window	Ctrl+M

Continued

Table B.3 *(continued)*

Description	Mac	PC
Zoom iTunes Window	Option+Click Zoom Control in Upper-Left Corner of iTunes Window	Shift+Double-Click Title Bar
Resize iTunes Window (With Preview)	⌘+Drag Resize Box in Lower-Right Corner of iTunes Window	N/A
Open iTunes Preferences	⌘+Comma (,)	Ctrl+Comma (,)
Open View Options Window for Selected Source	⌘+J	Ctrl+J
Expand or Collapse Triangles in Radio's Stream List	⌘+Click Triangle	Ctrl+Click Triangle
Hide or Show Artist and Album Columns	⌘+B	Ctrl+B
Hide or Show Song Artwork	⌘+G	Ctrl+G

Table B.4
Visualizer Shortcuts

Description	Mac	PC
Turn Visualizer On or Off	⌘+T	Ctrl+T
Full-Screen Visualizer On or Off	⌘+F	Ctrl+F
View Options for Visual Effects (While Playing)	Press ?, Then Press Indicated Key to Select Option	Press ?, Then Press Indicated Key to Select Option

Table B.5
iTunes Music Store Shortcuts

Description	Mac	PC
Go to Next Page in Music Store	⌘+Right Bracket ( ])	Ctrl+Right Bracket ( ])
Go to Previous Page in Music Store	⌘+Left Bracket ( ])	Ctrl+Left Bracket ([ )

Glossary

AAC (Advanced Audio Coding)
Apple's preferred compression format, and replacement for MP3, which is the default format for iTunes and the iTunes Music Store (the Music Store uses proprietary Apple Digital Rights Management extensions, known as FairPlay) for Macintosh. This format is part of the MPEG-4 specifications and offers an improved, more efficient form of audio compression that surpasses MP3, even at lower bit rates. For example, a 96 Kbps AAC file often sounds better than an MP3 file encoded at 128 Kbps or higher.

AIFF (Audio Interchange File Format)
Uncompressed audio file format for the Macintosh, which provides CD-quality sound (essentially the same as a WAV file on a PC). Audio files on a CD are uncompressed and can be ripped onto your hard drive in the AIFF format for the best possible sound quality.

AirPort Express
Mobile WiFi base station (802.11g) that can be used to play music streamed from iTunes anywhere in the house or to extend a wireless connection to your laptop computer.

AirPort Extreme
WiFi base station that provides up to 54 Mbps (802.11g) wireless network access or acts as a wireless bridge in an existing network.

AirTunes
Feature of AirPort Express that allows iTunes music to be played anywhere in the house using a wireless network and a connection to a home stereo system or powered speakers.

Apple Lossless
Apple's own codec for uncompressed, CD-quality audio files with half the space requirements of the original file. Excellent choice for audiophiles concerned about maintaining perfect audio quality while utilizing less space.

AppleScript

Apple's own scripting language, which automates the actions of a Macintosh and its applications. These scripts can reduce the number of time-consuming and repetitive tasks you perform, such as re-labeling a large number of folders, and can be used to enhance the functionality of existing software, such as iTunes.

Audible

Audible.com's proprietary audio format for distributing protected audiobook files. Audible files encoded in Formats 2, 3, or 4 can be read by an iPod. Format 2 provides the smallest files at the lowest quality, while Format 3 and 4 provide progressively better audio quality and file sizes.

Bitrate

The amount of bits, or data, allocated for the compression and playback of digital files over time. Also known as the *data rate,* or the rate at which data is transmitted. The bit rate used to encode an audio file will determine its file size and quality to a large degree.

CDDB (CD Database)

Online CD database (also called *Gracenote*), which is used to automatically download song titles and other information for music ripped from a CD and imported into iTunes.

Click Wheel

An iPod's touch-sensitive navigation wheel (not available on iPod shuffle), which allows you to easily scroll through playlists and songs, and make selections using a single finger.

Codec

The method used to compress and decompress data, such as the AAC and MP3 audio formats. The name is derived from the combination of the words compression and decompression.

Constant bit rate (CBR)

Data encoded and played back at a single, fixed bit rate. Simple and complex passages of audio and video files are treated the same, which provides a consistent, but less efficient, form of compression.

Data rate

See Bitrate.

Dock

Desktop cradle for easily charging an iPod and connecting it to powered speakers via a stereo line out. iPod photo offers a dock that includes an S-Video output for connecting to a TV.

Dock connector

Beginning with 4G iPods, a special, thin connector at the bottom of all iPod devices (with the exception of iPod shuffle), which provides power for charging the device, as well as data transfer through special FireWire and USB 2.0 cables.

DRM (Digital Rights Management)

Software feature that allows for the control of copyrighted material, such as songs downloaded from the iTunes Music Store, including limitations on the amount of times a song can be copied or the number of devices it can be played on. DRM software is incorporated into legally downloaded iTunes music files.

FairPlay

The name of Apple's proprietary DRM used with iTunes Music Store files.

FireWire

Extremely fast digital connection developed by Apple to interface devices, such as a computer and an iPod (also known as IEEE 1394 or i.Link). A standard FireWire connection provides data transfers of up to 400 Mbps, which speeds the transfer of an entire music collection or large data files. A single FireWire cable provides power to a device in addition to the transfer of data. An 800 Mbps variety with twice the speed is available, although it isn't available for use with an iPod.

Firmware

Software or other data that is part of the ROM (Read-Only Memory) on a hardware device, such as an iPod. Firmware is necessary to the operation of a device, although it can be updated to improve a device's functionality or to add new features.

Flash Memory

Digital storage on a memory chip that is written or erased in a "flash," using non-moving parts, which makes them immune to skipping (as opposed to a hard drive with a spinning mechanism). iPod shuffle utilizes flash memory, as do memory cards for digital cameras and other portable devices.

Gracenote

See CDDB.

IEEE

See FireWire.

iMix

Playlists published to the iTunes Music Store, which can be created by any user and browsed or rated by others looking to find new music.

iPhoto

iLife application that performs photo storage and editing tasks for Mac users, including the importing of images to be used for display on iPod photo. Windows users can use either Photoshop Elements 3 or Photoshop Album software.

iSync

Synchronization software that allows devices, such as iPods, cell phones, and PDAs, to communicate and update calendar appointments and other information when connected to a computer. Safari bookmarks and other data can be updated through iSync and a .Mac account as well. If you are using iTunes 4.8 or later, iTunes manages calendar and contact synchronization with an iPod rather than iSync.

iTunes

iLife application that imports, sorts, and otherwise manages music for playback on the computer desktop or with an iPod.

LED (Light Emitting Diode)

Light source that provides a backlight for the iPod's liquid crystal display. The standard LED color in an iPod is blue-white.

MP3 (MPEG 1, Audio Layer 3)

The most popular codec for the storage and transfer of music as digital files over the Internet. MP3 files use a lossy form of compression that removes inaudible frequencies of sound to reduce the amount of data necessary to encode. Information is sacrificed, creating files that are considerably smaller, yet (depending on the bit rate used) imperceptibly different from CD audio tracks (at least to the average listener).

On-the-go playlists

Playlists on your iPod created by selecting songs without using iTunes or your home computer.

Party shuffle

Play mode that generates a random mix of songs from a playlist or your entire iTunes library.

Playlist

An organized collection or combination of songs arranged in a list that can be burned to a CD, published online, or instantly accessed through the music menu on an iPod or the Source list in iTunes. Playlists point to songs in your library and may be rearranged, deleted, or otherwise edited without affecting the storage space on your hard drive or altering the original song file.

Podcasting

iPod broadcasts—a replacement for traditional radio broadcasts, which includes audio files that can be manually downloaded or updated automatically through an RSS feed and uploaded to an iPod.

RSS

A format for presenting information from a Web site as a feed. These *feeds,* or streams of information, allow an iPod to display content from the Web as text, since Web pages cannot be viewed on an iPod. RSS is typically used with an *aggregator,* which is an application that collects and updates multiple feeds. This format is particularly useful for information from news-oriented sites and personal weblogs.

Smart playlists

Playlists that are automatically generated and designed to suit your mood based on a selection of preferences, such as genre, the year an album was released, or the number of times a song has been played.

USB (Universal Serial Bus)

Computer interface for connecting a variety of peripherals such as keyboards, printers, and other devices, like an iPod or digital camera. USB 2.0 is the latest standard (backward compatible with an earlier 1.1 version), with a fast data transfer speed of 480 Mbps. PC users can use USB 2.0 to connect an iPod to their computer.

Variable bit rate (VBR)

Data that is encoded and transmitted at varying bit rates. Bits are allocated as needed, based on the complexity of audio and video information, which provides a more efficient form of compression.

WAV

The standard, uncompressed audio file format for PCs using the Windows operating system. These files are the basis for CD-quality sound and are the equivalent of AIFF files on a Mac.

WiFi

A wireless technology for connecting computer devices through the use of radio waves, without the need for cables to join them. AirPort Express uses WiFi to receive music sent from your desktop computer and AirPort Extreme base station.

WMA (Windows Media Audio)

The proprietary, compressed Microsoft audio format, designed for the Windows Media Player and similar to MP3 and AAC audio formats. WMAs require conversion through iTunes or another application to be played on an iPod (as long as they don't include DRM). This conversion is available only in the Windows version of iTunes.

Index

Continued